AROUND THE BANKS OF PIMLICO

Born in 1931, Máirín Johnston grew up in the heart of the Liberties, where her family on her mother's side had lived since 1850 and on her father's side since 1680. She attended St Brigid's National School, the Coombe, until she was 14 years of age. Until her marriage in 1952, she worked in various shirt factories and in Jacob's Biscuit Factory. Her main interests are music, politics, literature, the women's movement and social history. She is the mother of two girls and two boys.

First published in 1985 by
Attic Press,
44 East Essex Street,
Dublin 2.

Johnston, Máirín
  Around the banks of Pimlico.
  1. Dublin (Dublin) — Social life and customs.
  I. Title
  941.8'35081 DA995.D75
  ISBN 0-946211-16-7
  ISBN 0-946211-15-9 Pbk

Cover Design: Susanne Linde.
Typesetting: Phototype-Set Ltd., Dublin.
Printing: O'Brien Promotions, Dublin.

The publisher gratefully acknowledges the assistance of the copyright owners of illustration material reproduced in this book, in particular Colin Conroy, *Cork Examiner,* Fergal Costello, Earl of Meath, *Irish Times,* Ailín Johnston, Máirín Johnston, Liam Kennedy, Johnny Malone, Liam C. Martin, Barry Mason, National Library, Royal Society of Antiquaries, Johnson Collection, RTE.

AROUND THE BANKS OF PIMLICO

'No one else excites the imagination the way Máirín Johnston does as she guides us through four generations of life in one of Dublin's most celebrated and colourful streets.

Máirín Johnston

Attic Press, Dublin.

ACKNOWLEDGEMENTS

Credit for the idea that this history be written must go to Ita Gannon and Tommy Weldon, who in May 1980 asked me to speak at a seminar on 'Growing Up in Pimlico'. The weekend seminar was organised by the Dublin History Workshop and was held in St Catherine's Church, Thomas Street.

I am deeply indebted to the staffs of the various libraries who gave me every assistance during my research particularly to Ms Mary Clarke, Dublin City Archivist and Ms Paula Howard, Librarian in the Gilbert Library, Pearse Street whose kindness and help were invaluable in locating important information.

My gratitude to Eamonn Mac Thomais for his sound advice and to John Gallagher of the Liberties Association for his patience and encouragement.

At St Catherine's and St James, South Circular Road, the Rev Canon John Crawford gave me every assistance by allowing me to examine old church registers for family births, marriages and deaths and the Rev Fogarty of St Catherine's, Meath Street very generously gave me one of the carved frames of the stations which had been made by my father.

Eddie McEvoy of Deegan Photographs, Leeson Street was most helpful in providing old photographs and in copying and enlarging. My thanks also to Barry Mason Photographic Ltd., and to Liam Kennedy, Donnolly Centre, Cork Street.

Johnny Malone, a neighbour from Pimlico went out of his way to provide me with rare and valuable photographs for which I express my deepest gratitude. My thanks also to my childhood pals, Breda (Dowling) and Tommy Phelan for the photo of the class of '38 in School Street School.

A special word of thanks to the Earl of Meath and Mr Pat Houlihan of Kilorglin who were extremely trusting and generous in lending me old rare photographs to copy, and to Fergal Costello for his slides and photographs

For family history I wish to thank my brother Paddy and my cousin Bridie Kerrigan who helped to roll back the years.

Most of all I wish to thank my brother, Stephen, who for five years helped with the research, checked sources and provided valuable information. Without his constant assistance and encouragement this book would never have been written.

Máirín Johnston, 1985.

We gratefully acknowledge the support of the following businesses in the Liberties for their financial support which helped to make the production of this book possible. **Stephenson Associates, Burdocks, John Gaynor & Co., Ryan Bros.** (public house), **The Clock** (public house), **The Pimlico Tavern, The Old Dublin Restaurant, Jewels** (Meath Street jewellers), The Brazen Head and the Lord Edward Restaurant.

DEDICATION

To Úna, Fergus, Ailín and Gareth.

ILLUSTRATIONS

CONTENTS

FAMILY TREE

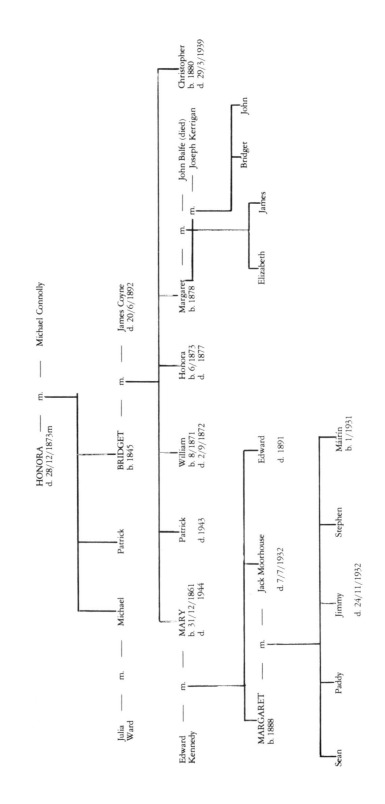

Abbey and Court-House of St Thomas

Pimlico is a long, narrow street which stretches from the top of the Coombe at Ardee Street up to the corners of Thomas Court Bawn and Marrowbone Lane. On its approach to the Bawn it takes a sudden sharp turn to the left just beyond Meath Place and the Banks. It is one of the oldest streets in the Earl of Meath's Liberties and in medieval times it was called Donoure Street. When the French Huguenots and the English woollen workers settled in the Liberties in the late 1660s, the Earl of Meath leased out parts of his land to them, on which they built their own very distinctive style of housing. The English immigrants gave to some of the streets in the area names like Pimlico, Tripoli, Marrowbone (Marylebone) Lane and Spitalfields. When Donoure Street became Pimlico, the short part of it at the turn after Meath Place became Tripoli, sometimes spelt Tripilo. The name Tripoli went out of use after the Artisans' Dwellings were completed at this end of Pimlico in 1885, although older inhabitants of the street used it even when I was growing up.

The street and its environs are steeped in history and in earlier times it had close associations with royalty. Once upon a time kings and nobility were as familiar in the neighbourhood as were the weavers of the 1670s and the Guinness workers are today.

After the fall of Dublin, during the Norman invasion, the city became the centre of English rule in Ireland. Shortly after this, on 29 December 1170, King Henry II of England had Thomas à Becket, Archbishop of Canterbury, murdered in Canterbury Cathedral. Two years later Thomas à Becket was canonised and Henry suffered terrible pangs of conscience, and in order to make reparation for the murder he decided to build an abbey in his honour.

So, on his peregrinations around the western suburbs of Dublin one day, he clapped his eye on a nice piece of pasture land half-way between Thomas Street and Donoure Street. It was obviously ideal for the purpose he had in mind, and without a second thought he said, 'Upon this land I will build my abbey,' and so he did in 1177. The abbey was a very extensive and noble pile of buildings and occupied all the land between what is now Hanbury Lane and South Earl Street. To the south-west of the abbey was a large bawn or courtyard which was watered by the city watercourse, from which the abbots were entitled by their charter to have supply *gratis,* for domestic purposes and as a supply for their water-mills.

The abbey was dedicated to the Order of the Canons of the Congregation of St Victor. It was one of the earliest monuments of the new influence of English rule and was a special object of royal favour. It was not only un-Irish in character, it was most definitely anti-Irish, and operated within its walls the principle of 'No Irish need apply'. It functioned as an ecclesiastical fort of English power, under the direct control of the king and was nourished by him as a useful agent in the affairs of State.

The abbots, who were appointed and held office subject to royal approval, were *ex officio* members of the Irish privy council and peers of the Irish parliament, besides exercising judicial functions at the court of the abbey.

King John, son of Henry II, on one of his visits to the abbey, constituted it and its lands a liberty in 1210, by the name of the Liberty of Thomas Court and Donoure. This meant that the districts were exempt from the jurisdiction of the mayor of the city. The abbot had full authority in the districts, from the execution of criminals to weights and measures of bread and brew.

The court-house of the abbey stood in Thomas Court Bawn, and the marshalsea was in Marrowbone Lane. In its time the abbey was the scene of many comings and goings of lord lieutenants and kings, who were entertained within its walls and also held court there.

But if one Henry gave us the abbey another Henry took it away, for in 1539 Henry VIII suppressed the monasteries in Ireland. The last abbot of the abbey was Henry Duff, who was granted a pension of £42 Irish, payable out of the tithes of several rectories.

At this time the king's under treasurer was William Brabazon, who was held in good favour, and so, as a small token of appreciation for his services, Henry VIII gave him a present of the abbey, court-house and liberty. According to historical data the grant occurred on two separate occasions, one on 31 March 1539, when the side of the monastery with a malt mill, a wood mill and the double mills, one carucate of land called Donouer (Donore), ten acres of meadow, two of pasture and ten of underwood, rear of the Abbey, were granted to William Brabazon, for ever, by military service at the annual rent of eighteen shillings and sixpence. In 1545 these lands and possessions were granted to the same person with the site and circuit of the monastery of Thomas Court, the church, the churchyard, and all the tenths of the premises, and all jurisdictions and liberties, etc., spiritual and temporal, to hold *in capite* by the twentieth part of a knight's fee at the yearly rent of one pound fourteen and elevenpence. The rest of the abbey's lands were distributed among other loyal servants of the king.

Sir William Brabazon died when his son Edward was only three years old. In about 1578 he erected a new court-house. Edward was advanced to the dignity of baron, by the title of Lord Brabazon, Baron of Ardee, in the county of Louth by privy seal at Newmarket in 1613/14 and by patent at Dublin on 19 July 1616. He died on 7 August 1625.

He was succeeded by his son William, second Baron of Ardee, who by privy seal was made Earl of Meath on 28 March 1627 and by patent at Dublin on 16 April 1627. Thereafter, the area was known as the Earl of Meath's Liberties. In the rebellion of 1641, the earl suffered losses of up to £700 by the wasting and demolition of houses on his land in Thomas Court. Fences and fortifications were made through it for the defence of the city of Dublin and his house at Kilruddery was also burned.

The first Earl of Meath made Thomas Court his city home. He died in Thomas Court on 19 December 1651 and is buried in St Catherine's Church, Thomas Street. He had one son called Edward who became the second earl, and who lived in Thomas Court as earl for twenty-four years. He died at sea between Holyhead and Beaumaris on 25 March 1675. He was the last Earl of Meath to reside in the Liberties. After his death the great house in Thomas Court was demolished and its orchards, gardens and woods were all cleared away and laid out for building. Somewhere between 1610 and 1630 the monastic buildings had already disappeared.

The court-house in Thomas Court Bawn remained and continued to perform its functions, weighing and measuring and suing for debts before a seneschal, but gradually the considerable powers of the court-house dwindled as improvements in city management and governing were made, until finally, in 1859, an Act of Parliament abolished its powers altogether.

A description of the court-house in the *Irish Builder* of 1893 tells us that it was a brick building, having a stone front towards Tripoli, from which was the principal entrance. It was sixty feet in depth by thirty feet in width and was two storeys high. The upper storey contained the residence of the caretaker and the lower one was fitted up for the court-house, with offices for the seneschal, the registrar and other officers.

The court-house, or manor court as it is sometimes called, had an interesting and varied history. While it carried out its functions as a court-house, it was also used for other purposes, as when, in 1760, it was fitted up as the place of worship for the parishioners of St Catherine's during the rebuilding of their parish church, the architect for which was John Smyth. The church was completed in 1769, so obviously the court-house was a place of worship for a long time.

St Catherine's had occasion to use the court-house again in 1786, when the Rev R. Powell established the second Sunday school in Ireland. Because of the huge numbers of children wishing to avail of the Sunday school education it was necessary to divide the children, so the girls continued to attend at St Catherine's but the boys went to the manor house in Thomas Court Bawn. This Sunday school was the fore-runner of the famous Dublin Free Dayschool later known as School Street School.

In 1807 the seneschal of the court-house was the renowned Dublin historian, Rev James Whitelaw, who was also the vicar of St Catherine's Church. He compiled a census of the area in 1798, which recorded the overcrowding, distress and extreme poverty of the people in the tenements. Later he established the Meath Charitable Loan which gave some relief to the starving weavers and which was interest-free. The woollen industry was in a sad state of decline, due to the embargoes and duties imposed by the British on exports abroad and to the import of foreign silk which glutted the Dublin market. Whitelaw died on 4 February 1813, from typhoid fever, which he contracted while visiting a sick parishioner.

Manor Courthouse before its demolition in 1897

A series of letters appeared in *The Freeman's Journal* in 1816, written by 'Viator' who had an address in Thomas Court. They were written to the Right Hon Robert Peel, chief secretary to the lord lieutenant of Ireland and related to the improvement of the district of the metropolis, and principally to the Earl of Meath's Liberties, 'by making therein, Wide and Convenient Streets'. In his letters 'Viator' suggested that the Commissioners of Wide Streets should meet, not at the Royal Exchange, which was the usual meeting-place, but somewhere else in the south-west part of the before- mentioned district. He recommended the Court-house of St Thomas, 'not yet fallen into ruin, and with the use thereof, I presume that the Earl of Meath would willingly accommodate the Commissioners for a purpose so beneficial to his wretched tenantry. This place of meeting, I suggest, as from its windows the most desirable and beneficial improvements would offer themselves for their consideration.' He further goes on to point out that the Liberties contain nothing that deserves the name of a public building except the two churches of St Catherine and St Luke, the Fever Hospital and School Street School.

In 1825 the Earl of Meath spent the vast sum of £200 repairing the court-house and putting on a new roof, so obviously 'Viator's' remarks weren't entirely wasted. But as a court-house, its days were numbered. The Act of Parliament of 1859 abolished all manor courts and brought to an end the authority of the seneschal who had reigned within the Liberties with power almost equal to the lord mayor of the city.

Between 1860 and 1873, the court-house is listed in *Thom's Directory* as vacant, but in 1874 it took on a new lease of life when James Darbyshire, clog- and shoemaker, opened up his factory. He remained there for ten years until he died, and then it was taken over by Thomas Higgins. It then opened up as a playhouse, known as the Thomas Court Theatre, but by now its very existence was threatened and its appearance was more wretched and dilapidated. In 1896 the land on which the court-house stood was sold by the Earl of Meath to the Corporation for fifty pounds. It had by now fallen very much into decay and no one seemed to care about it any more. There was pressure on the Corporation to widen the road in the Bawn, as there was only eighteen feet of carriageway, which included the footpath, and it was used very much by heavy traffic from the various distillers, brewers, tanners and other local industries.

So in 1897 the old manor court was levelled and fifteen feet of its site was added to the roadway. For the sake of acquiring such a small piece of land the only remaining building linking the area with its historic and noble past was demolished. The flank wall which divided the court-house from the adjoining dwelling house in Tripoli, which was No 35 Pimlico, where my family lived, was properly repaired and the remaining fifteen feet of the original depth of the court-house was allocated for the site of a memorial fountain. This was erected by the Earl and Countess of Meath and the opening ceremony was performed on 21 May 1898.

The last remaining traces of the court-house were demolished in the latter half of 1958 after Dublin Corporation acquired Nos 30–35 Pimlico for redevelopment.

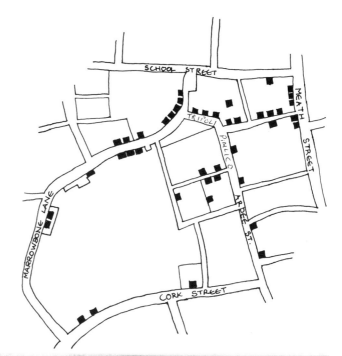

Map showing houses in which there had been outbreaks of fever and diseases (1871) and Trade Unionists, with banners and placards, assembling outside St Catherine's Church, Thomas Street in the early 1900s.

The Good Old Days

The old court-house in Thomas Court Bawn was still nearly a decade away from losing its manorial rights when my great-great-grandmother, Honora Connolly, first arrived in the Liberties in 1850. Like thousands of other poverty-stricken peasants she had been forced to leave her native place, Gort in County Galway, because of famine and destitution. Her husband, Michael Connolly had died and Honora was left to fend for herself and her young family. With some of her neighbours she took the road east and headed for Dublin where she found accommodation in No 52 Marrowbone Lane, over a public house owned by Grace Harrower.

Marrowbone Lane meanders snake-like from Thomas Court Bawn to Cork Street. The name is said to be a corruption of Marylebone and, like other street names in the area it dates from the time English woollen workers and the followers of William III or William of Orange settled in the district. Many of the houses in the area were built during this period and were nick-named Dutch Billys, after the king.

By the time Honora took up residence these houses were already over a century and a half old and were in a very decrepit condition. Although a Public Health Act had been passed in 1848, no improvements had been made in the insanitary conditions in which working-class people were forced to live. In 1866 this Act was increased in stringency and was made compulsory in 1874.

A description of the housing conditions in Marrowbone Lane at the time was printed in *The Freeman's Journal* of 15 September 1871 some years after improvements ought to have taken place. The reporter was accompanied by a Dr Grimshaw, and they both made a tour of the Liberties, starting at Cork Street Fever Hospital. The report states:

> Exactly at the corner of the Lane are two tenement houses at the junction of Cork Street. The first is miserable, tumble-down and wretched. I draw special attention to the second. It is a large house, three storeys high. A few miserable planks serve as an apology for a door. The great window places stand bare and open, admitting winds of the heavens, the rain and the rays of the summer sun. Half the roof has been blown or has fallen off the house and in this ruin there are human beings residing. The houses look back on a yard, ankle-deep in filth and garbage, with foul sewer, manure heap and every conceivable abomination. Passing from this frightful spot we come to the first dairy-yards. These dairy-yards are simply fever nests. There is an open space on the left surrounded everywhere by houses. The space is literally swarming with cess pools and manure heaps and a thick black ooze distilled from the latter, trickled in streams to the doors of the houses. An open watercourse skirted one corner of the square. In this neighbourhood the Poddle is an open drain. It contains water which is little more than sewage, stagnant, sluggish, offensive in smell and appearance. A woman took a canful of water from this putrid stream as we watched. Further on was the Corporation Manure Yard, more than an acre of ground with many tons of manure. In the corner was the disinfectant apparatus. Neal's Court which is a square rather than a court is occupied by wretched tenements. No where in our journey did we see the evil of overcrowding more strikingly manifest. The square is ankle-deep in filth of every kind. In the centre is a reeking ashpit which seemed not to have been emptied for months. Goats, pigs and hens swarm about. Even on dry days it is difficult to walk through the sluch, and the stench is appalling. The unsavoury quarters of Tripoli and Pimlico presented similar objectionable features.

In 1885 Dr Grimshaw paid another visit to Marrowbone Lane and to his utter horror he found these same conditions still existed — even the goats, pigs and hens described in the report were there and but for the long interval which had elapsed between 1871 and 1885 they might almost have been recognised as the same animals.

The house in which Honora lived was almost opposite the junction where Forbes's Lane branches off up to the Grand Canal. It was a lively spot with plenty of activity on the canal, which was used a great deal by Guinness's barges and boats carrying turf and other commodities. Nearby was Jameson and Robertson the distillers, and further down was Cannon's the tanners, where Honora's eldest son, Michael, eventually got a job. The marshalsea of the old court-house was almost opposite to Nixon's the oil manufacturer, and in it lived Mr Lloyd, the marshal. Here and there were little huxter shops all clutter and darkness, cottages and dairies, and as well as goats, pigs and hens there were horses and cows, stables and haysheds. There was a constant stream of traffic to and from the canal and the various industries and distillers. The noise of the horse-drawn traffic on the cobble-stones as the carts with wooden wheels trundled along and the endless day and night animal noises meant that the dwellers in the overcrowded tenements got very little sleep.

Honora got herself a job as a domestic help and the children, in keeping with the times, also got work tending livestock and poultry, milking cows and delivering milk.

The first of Honora's children to marry was Michael. He married Julia Ward, who lived three doors away in No 55 Marrowbone Lane, on 16 January 1854, in St Catherine's Church, Meath Street. The next son, Patrick, emigrated to Pennsylvania, where he is reputed to have made his fortune digging coal. He returned only once on holiday, looking for all the world like a pirate, with a gold earring dangling from his left ear down to his shoulder. His appearance caused a great sensation in the street and was the subject of much comment within the family for years afterwards. He hasn't been seen or heard of since.

Irish was the language of the home, and as some of their old neighbours from Gort lived nearby as well as native Irish speakers from other parts of the country the language was kept alive in the area for many years. It wasn't until my granny started school in School Street, where the teaching was through English, that the Irish language began to take a secondary place in the home. In order to survive in the developing industrial setting it was necessary to get an education and this was only obtainable through English.

Honora's youngest child, Bridget, married James Coyne from No 2 Tripoli on 14 January 1861, also in St Catherine's. These were my great-grandparents. Bridget was only sixteen years of age, but James's prospects looked good. He was a bellman and owned his own horse and cart which he kept in a yard in Braithwaite Street, which has always been called Breffer Street by the locals. However, James was over-fond of the drop of porter and he drank as quickly as he earned, reducing the family circumstances to such an extent that Bridget had to get herself a job. She worked for many years in the house of a Protestant rector in Harold's Cross as a domestic, but she always gave herself the grand title of housekeeper.

Bridget's first child, Mary, my grandmother, was born on 31 December 1861 in No 2 Tripoli. On the day on which she was christened in St Catherine's either the priest or her godmother must have been drunk, because she was christened James after her father. This caused her no end of trouble in later life when she was required to produce certificates for official reasons. She was seventy years of age before the name was corrected to enable her to get the old-age pension. The next child, Patrick, was also born at this address on 4 October 1866.

In 1870 Bridget moved into No 1 Tripoli. At this time Honora came to live with her daughter, because her health was failing and all her children were now married. When William, Bridget's third child, was thirteen months old he became ill, and after two weeks of

Aunt Maggie, a weaver in Mitchells,
Brabazon Row, 1896.

sickness he died on 2 September 1872 from gastroenteritis. Nine months later Honora was born, but when she was only six months old Honora senior died from acute bronchitis on 23 December 1873. Young Honora had just reached her fourth birthday when she too became ill and after four days of sickness she died from croup.

These were very sad times for the family. The poverty, appalling housing, sickness, deaths and miscarriages were affecting Bridget's health. Mary was now sixteen years of age and was working as a monitor in School Street School. The hours suited her and enabled her to help her mother to rear the younger children.

Bridget and James were now convinced that No 1 Tripoli was an unlucky house to live in and they decided to get out at the earliest possible opportunity. This wasn't easy. The area was overcrowded and vacant rooms were hard to come by. Adding to the problem were the compulsory purchase orders which closed many of the tenements. These were deemed unfit for human habitation and were being demolished to facilitate the new development plans for the area. Perhaps Bridget's superstition about the house was well founded, because one day part of the outer wall caved in and all the tenants were left homeless.

A room was found in No 4 Tripoli, where Bridget's brother Michael and family already lived, and in the fulness of time Margaret was born in 1878, and the last child, Christopher, in 1880. Shortly after his birth the family was on the move again, this time up to the house at the corner of Tripoli right next door to the old court-house. Here they remained for the next seventy-eight years.

The Coombe Ragged School

When the great-great-granny Honora had been almost three years living in Marrowbone Lane, a knock came on her door one day, and there, standing on the landing was a man holding a bundle of books and leaflets in his hand. He explained to her, in a gentlemanly fashion, that he was from the Irish Church Missions to Roman Catholics and was going around all the neighbourhood in the hope of interesting the people in the work of the mission. He was happy to announce that in pursuance of their carrying out of God's work, a new ragged school for the poor of the district was being opened on the Coombe shortly. Honora wasn't able to follow the drift of his conversation, which was a little ploy she used when she didn't want to get involved with strange gentlemen at the door, but as soon as he discovered that she was an Irish speaker, he switched over to Irish without the slightest bit of bother.

The purpose of the school, he said, was to bring the message of the Gospel and the Scriptures to Roman Catholics who were especially ignorant of such knowledge. It was only through the Scriptures that men would be saved and the Roman Church had failed to supply to its members the true way of Salvation.

At this stage, Honora really hadn't a notion what he was on about, but as she didn't want to hurt his feelings she eventually took his leaflet and a copy of the Bible, both of which were in Irish. She promised that she would get the children to have a look over them as she wasn't too good at the reading. The leaflet was called 'A Voice From Heaven To The People Of Ireland' and was by the Rev A. Dallas.

After finding out that she was a poor widow with four children, the man said that she would be pleased to know that a hot breakfast would be given to the children every day before school began. With that he was gone, leaving her with all the particulars about the opening day.

As it happened, the only one of Honora's children who was attending school at that time was the youngest, Bridget, who was just eight years of age. She was attending School Street School and Honora was more than satisfied with the non-denominational education she was getting there.

Honora was not altogether unfamiliar with missionaries bearing gifts, because many mission stations had established themselves over in the west before the famine, but she had never heard of the Irish Church Missions to Roman Catholics before, for the very good reason that their arrival in Galway coincided with her departure to Dublin. Very soon, however, she was to hear a great deal about them and so too was the whole city of Dublin as well as other cities, notably Kilkenny.

Of all the evangelical missionary societies to come to Ireland none caused as much dissension, discord and division among the people and between the Catholic and Protestant clergy as did the Irish Church Missions to Roman Catholics. Much of the bigotry, sectarianism and rioting which resulted from their biblical crusade was due to the fanatical missionary zeal of their founder, the Rev Alexander Dallas. He was an Englishman who firmly believed that the Famine was an Act of God visited upon the Irish as punishment for their ignorance and superstition and their slavish adherence to a foreign power — the Church of Rome. His convictions filled him with a fanatical determination to save the people of Ireland from the hellish clutches of this idolatrous religions.

Before he got the Call and was converted to the Work of God, Mr Dallas had been an officer in the Napoleonic Wars. He came from a very wealthy family background and was a first cousin to Lord Byron, the poet. When he first took an interest in the salvation of the Irish he was Rector of Wonston, in Hampshire.

The Irish Church Missions was founded in 1846 and began its work in Connemara, but it wasn't until March 1849 that it was officially established as a society. The success of its crusade in the west encouraged the Rev Dallas to turn to the east and so, after two years, mission halls and schools were opened in Dublin. The first of these was in Townsend Street.

Before very long it was decided to extend the work into the Liberties. The Coombe, with its overcrowded tenements and poverty, was an obvious place to conduct the work of salvation,

> ... where the habitual sin of the people was drunkeness. It is this in many homes that makes food, fire and furniture scarce, banishes peace and comfort, and makes miserable the lives of little children. Their clothes are in rags and their bodies marked from beatings. One small street seems to be the Sodom of the district.'

So, on this fetid, fertile soil the seeds of salvation were to be soon sown.

Irish Church Missions Pamphlet 1876

Gather them in from the lanes and streets
Gather them in from their dark retreats
From the haunts of folly, from the dens of crime
Gather them in, in their early prime
Gather them in with a christian zeal
Gather them in for their country's weal
Gather them in with abundant store
Garnished in glory evermore.

The houses on the Coombe, which at one time had been inhabited by well-off weavers, were now occupied by the poor, many of them the descendants of those craft-workers.

As well as the dilapidated houses, the street was lined from top to bottom with huxter shops selling old nails, bits of iron, old wheels, carriage cushions, tables, chairs, boxes, cradles, iron pots, kettles and bedsteads, periwinkles, bones, heaps of potatoes and dripping; hand-me-down shops with sacks of rags, hanging inside and outside, old dresses, aprons, jackets and boots; shops with oranges, tapes, buttons, needles, fish, sugar-sticks and cockles.

With such a conglomeration of humans and objects the missionaries had a job trying to find a suitable premises for their school, but eventually, they managed to get accommodation in the Weavers' Hall, which, like all the other houses, was in a bad state of repair. Only the entrance hall and the large room upstairs could be rented but it was better than nothing.

Having acquired the premises, the missionaries set about informing the people about their crusade, so the agents, who were called town commissioners, were sent forth to announce the glad tidings of the salvation which was to come. 'At that time many poor people in Dublin found it hard to understand English,' so the missionaries took the precaution of sending Irish speakers. Taking advantage of the fact that the people were impoverished — many of them destitute — food and clothing were promised to all those who would attend. It was this method of combining charity with missionary work which earned them the description 'proselytisers'. Those who accepted their charity and renounced the Catholic faith were called 'soupers' and those who reverted to Catholicism were called 'jumpers'.

Go and seek the little wanderers from the crowded street
Give them shelter, food and raiment, warm their weary feet
Few their comforts, few their pleasures, life to them is drear
They could tell a tale of sorrow you would weep to hear
Go and seek the little wanderers, take them by the hand
Give them shelter, food and raiment, 'tis the Lord's command.

With the pre-publicity campaign completed, the dining-room of the Corporation of Weavers was transformed into a schoolroom, with the help of a few forms and desks, maps and diagrams. A washing tub was purchased for half a crown and ten and ninepence was spent on sundries, which included soap and scrubbing brushes. The missionaries obviously weren't taking any chances.

The opening day was 24 April 1853, but unfortunately there was no kitchen to prepare the promised food. However, when needs must the devil drives, so the children were given a piece of bread at 1 p.m. in lieu, which encouraged them to remain until 3 p.m. The bread must have gone down very well and the news spread like wildfire, because in a few days the room was full of 'half-naked boys and girls'. It wasn't long before Sunday school started, to which the parents as well as the children were invited. Fifty parents came the first Sunday but the attendance increased so much on the following Sundays that the adult classes had to be divided. Two special classes for Irish speakers were introduced and before many weeks had elapsed the doors of the Weavers' Hall had to be closed at 3.15 p.m. leaving hundreds outside unable to get in.

The value of conveying the message of the Gospel in Irish to the Irish-speaking population had long since been recognised and tackled. 'Neglect of the language had led to the perpetuation of a large and bigoted Roman community and it added to and tended to keep up and increase political differences.' In 1818, the Irish Society for Promoting the Education of the Native Irish through the Medium of Their Own Tongue had been formed, and clergymen of the Established Church and missionary workers were encouraged to learn Irish, 'so that they might converse with their parishioners in the language with which they were familiar'.

Most of the people in the Liberties at that time were Roman Catholics, but there was a fair sprinkling of Protestants of English and Huguenot descent. Some of these had married into Catholic families, as my father's people had done, resulting in families of mixed persuasions. They had been weaving more than silk and poplin since the late 1600s — two hundred years of living and working together, suffering alike the hardships and unemployment brought about by the demise of the local industries and crafts, had woven together the fabric of their lives. It was this inter-relationship of different cultures, religions and origins which made the people in the Liberties different from other communities.

The advent of the Irish Church Missions in their midst and the methods which they employed to entice the Roman Catholics away from their faith caused panic and anger among the Catholic clergy at all levels. As soon as the local parish priest in Francis Street, Father Matthew Flanagan, saw his flock going in their hundreds to the Weavers' Hall to get the bit of grub and being told that their priests were denying them the Gospel of Christ and thereby keeping them in a state of ignorance and superstition, he decided to take action. He opened a Catholic ragged school in New Row, up over a shop in a tenement house. It consisted of four small rooms, with fifteen forms and no desks. The two teachers, James Shiel and Anne Fox, had no qualifications or experience. It was clearly a makeshift arrangement and it failed to attract the Catholic children, so better accommodation was sought and was found in Park Street West, just off Hanover Street.

By contrast, the Irish Church Missions ragged school was going from strength to strength. By November the numbers had risen to 472. The staircase and entrance hall were now being used for classes and crowds were still being turned away. Another house in New Row, also in a bad state of repair, was rented and was used to accommodate the girls and infants, while the boys remained at the Weavers' Hall. In next to no time the numbers in New Row rose to 500. The floor gave way and had to be propped up and the walls had to be supported. It was feared that a serious accident would take place, so careful consideration was given to the possibilities of building a new school.

IRISH   CHURCH   MISSIONS.

Twenty-sixth Anniversary.

THE ANNUAL SERMONS

IN AID OF THIS SOCIETY, WILL BE PREACHED (D.V.)

On SUNDAYS, APRIL 11th and 18th, 1875,

Irish Church Missions Leaflet.

The money was pouring in from England to the Irish Church Missions, along with the enormous financial support which they received from wealthy people in Ireland. Through the munificence of the Earl of Meath, who granted a plot of his land at the corner of the Coombe and Skinners' Alley, now Newmarket Street, the hopes and dreams of the Irish Church Missions were more than realised. Within a year the new school was built and was ready for use. On Wednesday 11 February 1857 the Coombe Ragged School was publicly opened by the missionaries' founder, the Rev Alexander Dallas.

Meanwhile, the Catholic ragged school in Park Street West was floundering along. Two new teachers were employed, again with no testimonials. Catherine Moore taught sewing and Mary Nolan taught reading and writing. By August 1853 there were 212 males and 145 females on the books, but the daily attendance was only between nineteen and twenty-two pupils. On 8 May 1854 the District Inspector of National Schools, Mr MacDermott, paid a visit and in his brief report he wrote, 'This is a Ragged School — the children are of the most destitute class.'

The Catholic Church was becoming increasingly alarmed at the inroads being made into the Catholic community by the Irish Church Missions and it resolved to mobilise its forces. At that time there was active in Dublin an organisation called the Ladies' Association of Charity, which was founded in 1851. The president and secretary was a very pious woman named Margaret Louise Aylward, who was the daughter of a wealthy merchant prince from Waterford. Her work in the Ladies' Association brought her into contact with the poor and destitute people of the city, and inevitably it brought her into direct conflict with the missionaries:

> On her visits among the poor, Margaret observed that the poor people were also being visited by Protestant ladies who sought to induce the destitute mothers to give up their children to be reared in Mrs Smyly's Homes or to attend proselytising day-schools, and she saw at once the necessity of providing Catholic Homes for the children whose faith was in danger.

The proselytisers were vehemently denounced from the pulpits. Dr Paul Cullen, Archbishop of Dublin, issued a pastoral letter on 'The Vile System of Pecuniary Proselytism' in which he listed the names of a number of societies whom he accused of carrying out the work of pecuniary proselytism:

> ... they have recourse to bribes and gifts to obtain the perversion of the poor and destitute and especially of children. These ragged schools are purely aggressive, instituted for the purpose of depriving poor Catholic children of their faith.

And so the war began and the scene was set for the battle for the souls of the poor people of the Liberties. With the approval of her friend Dr Paul Cullen, Margaret Aylward set up the first systematic Catholic opposition to the advance of the proselytisers in 1856. Father Flanagan of St Nicholas in Francis Street had just died and his place was taken by a more active parish priest named Rev Edward (Canon) McCabe, whose nine years' administration in the parish was distinctly marked by his vigorous crusade against the missionaries.

An orphanage was founded under the patronage of St Brigid, and Margaret Aylward

> .... induced destitute mothers to entrust to her care their children whose faith was in danger. The children were sent down the country and placed in suitably selected religious families who were paid £5 or £6 per annum to bring them up in the humble manner in which the peasants of Ireland are accustomed to live. In this way the orphans acquire that love of God and that spirit of religion for which this country is distinguished and at the same time they become strong and vigorous like the other inhabitants of the country and are prepared to bear the hardships to which persons of their class are generally exposed to in life.

Coombe Ragged School, corner of Newmarket Street and the Coombe, opened 1857

Wednesday 11 February 1857 dawned bright, clear and sunny. Evergreens, flowers and flags decorated the pure white walls of the new Coombe Ragged School. About 311 boys and girls of all ages assembled in the afternoon in the lower classrooms anxiously awaiting the feast, consisting of tea and cakes, which was being laid out for them upstairs. A greater number would have come, but only those who had attended for the last fortnight were admitted. There was also a crowded attendance of ladies, gentlemen and clergy, including the Hon and Very Revs the Deans of Christchurch and St Patrick's Cathedrals, the Dean of the Chapter Royal and Rev Mr Stanford. The Rev Alex Dallas briefly addressed the assembly and the children entertained with some hymns which they had learned to the tunes played every day on St Patrick's Bells, 'tunes all the Coombe people knew like "Rock of Ages", and when the children sing their parents are delighted to find words to the tunes so constantly sounded in their ears.'

Much to the relief of the missionaries, the day passed off without incident. They had been very apprehensive beforehand, and with justification, for between 1853 and 1857, the atmosphere on the Coombe and in the adjoining streets had become highly charged and explosive on several occasions. Scenes of mob violence, stone-pelting, abusive and sectarian name-calling and even kidnappings had become commonplace. The Irish Church Missions accused the Catholic Church of 'open and violent persecution' and the Catholic Church accused the missionaries of 'shocking recklessness towards the religion and outraged feelings of their unoffending Catholic fellow citizens.'

To watch over and check the progress of the missionaries, Cardinal Cullen appointed a general committee consisting of all the parish priests of the city, the heads of religious orders and some members of the clergy. Local committees were formed and a general collection was made on the feast of SS Peter and Paul to enable the general committee to build more schools for the children. The missionaries complained that these schools were always sited close to theirs. Lapsed Catholics were sometimes denounced from the pulpit by name but this was condemned by a resolution of the Catholic bishops in 1854.

On 25 March 1857 two incidents took place in Francis Street and High Street Chapels and the missionaries were accused of perpetrating a sacrilege. On 30 March, shortly before the Sunday school opened, crowds gathered on the Coombe and as the children arrived they were carried off forcibly to the Catholic Ragged School. However, that afternoon, 340 people, adults and children, managed to get into the mission school, while about 2000 raged against them outside. Before leaving, the children sang:

> We won't give up the Bible for pleasure or for pain
> We'll buy the truth and sell it not, for all that we might gain
> Though men may try to take our prize by guile or cruel might
> We'd suffer all that men can do, and God defend the right.

All through April the teachers from the ragged school were attacked, thrown in the mud, had their bonnets knocked off and were sometimes obliged to hide in shops. Eventually they had to travel to and fro in cabs.

Then on 12 May a most alarming riot took place on the Coombe. Fr McCabe decided to put a stop to the 'mischief and evil-doing of the proselytisers' and he arranged for a mission with the Vincentian Fathers, headed by Father Kavanagh, one of the greatest missionaries of his day. Devotions had just ended when a man named Joe Redmond from No 3 Patrick Street, who wasn't quite the full shilling, got up on to the altar-rails and began to act in a manner which the people didn't like. Someone shouted that he was a 'souper' and the crowd in the church dragged him out into the chapel yard. A man named Madine went to his assistance and both were so badly beaten that they had to be taken to hospital. An immense and excited crowd gathered from the four quarters of the Liberties and they marched down Francis Street and around the Coombe to the Weavers' Hall and smashed all the windows, then on to the old school in New Row where they did likewise. Some even went to St Bride's in Bride Street and then they attacked the new ragged school, where they knocked out not only the windows but also the teeth of Mr Holden, the headmaster.

Sixteen persons, male and female, some of them only fourteen years of age, were brought before the court. All were given fines or imprisonment. The poor unfortunate lunatic was charged with causing a disturbance but the court was told that his case couldn't be investigated until he had recovered sufficiently from his beatings.

One day a woman named Anne Fagan saluted the schoolmaster of St Nicholas Without School, which had no connection with the Coombe Ragged School, with the couplet,

> Souper, souper ring the bell
> Souper, souper go to hell.

She was arrested, taken into custody and fined a pound. Another day a local ballad-singer named Martin Power was arrested for creating a disturbance in Back Lane. His crime was that he was selling ballad-sheets embellished with pictorial caricatures which were of a grossly inflammatory character and was singing a ballad entitled 'The Divil Among the Soupers'.

In spite of the organised campaign against them, the Irish Church Missions continued to flourish. Every morning hordes of children packed the schoolhouse for the cocoa and bread and stayed on afterwards for the Bible classes. 'Many who come first seeking the bread that perisheth, find the Bread of Life and eat to the satisfying of the Soul's Hunger.' Often the children were taken from the school through the interference of the priest, who would call to their homes and sometimes they would wait outside the school taking their names and addresses.

The parish remained in a state of siege until 1858, when an extraordinary case of kidnapping hit the headlines which cast a cloud of doubt and suspicion over Margaret Aylward's work. A child of four years, named Mary Matthews, was committed by her dying father to the care of Margaret Aylward, to be reared as a Catholic. The child's mother, a Protestant, came to St Brigid's Orphanage to claim her child as she wished to bring her up at home. Margaret Aylward told the mother that she had sent Mary to a foster home from where she had been abducted and that no trace of her could be found.

Over a period of two years, Margaret Aylward was summoned repeatedly to the queen's bench to show cause why she didn't return the child to its mother. Finally, in November 1860, she was committed to Grangegorman Penitentiary for six months. Her imprisonment made legal history because she was the first person ever sent to jail for the successful concealment of a child. This scandal lost her much support among Catholics and she was left virtually alone. She was now fifty years of age and her imprisonment had broken her health. Nevertheless, on her release on 5 May 1861, she walked back to Eccles Street and resumed her work in the orphanage, helped by her loyal assistant, Ada Allingham, a cousin of the poet, William Allingham.

The publicity which had been given to the Mary Matthews case had helped to dampen the ardour of the extremist Catholics who were more concerned with saving souls than with alleviating hunger and want and so the level of violence against the ragged school subsided considerably. There were no more riots, although there continued to be isolated cases of provocation. Margaret Aylward set up a new religious community, and with the help of Fr John Gowan, CM, she eventually founded the Congregation of the Holy Faith in Glasnevin in 1867.

In 1869, the Rev Alexander Dallas died at the age of seventy-nine years. Although the

Established Church at the time didn't always see eye to eye with him, nevertheless a plaque in his honour was erected in St Patrick's Cathedral. It was in this year also that the Church of Ireland was disestablished and put on a footing with other churches.

Many children who attended the Coombe Ragged School during these years were totally destitute. They slept rough, in doorways, sheds, parks and on the landings of tenement houses. Night shelters allowed them to stay only for a fortnight at a time after which they had to move on as the shelters weren't intended to be treated as homes. Poor and homeless children were treated with the utmost cruelty by society and were imprisoned simply for being poor and homeless. In order not to lose their pupils, who were disappearing at the rate of twelve a week, the Irish Church Missionaries decided to build a boys' home on the Coombe. This and further improvements and extensions were carried out in 1870.

Whereas in the early days instruction had been purely religious, the children were now learning reading, writing and arithmetic. The English language was now replacing Irish in the homes of the native Irish speakers and the children in the ragged schools were being denied any sense of national identity. My granny, who was nine years of age at this time, remembered that the general consensus of opinion in the Liberties was that the children in the ragged school were regarded as cannon-fodder for the British Army and cheap if not slave labour for wealthy farmers.

The Catholic ragged school in Park Street was making steady progress and was attracting more children. By 1886, the numbers had risen to 350 and a more suitable school building was being sought. Through the generosity of Mr Myres, who lived on the Coombe, Margaret Aylward, now Mother Agnes in religion, was able to start a building project. Two large houses beside the new school were purchased; one served as a convent and the other as a secondary school which was known as St Philomena's Secondary School for young ladies and little boys.

In April 1887 350 little pupils marched proudly down from Park Street West into their new national school beside the firm of J.C. Parkes & Son. The national school was called St Brigid's and every day the sisters doled out a hot breakfast to the most destitute children. Two years later, on 11 October 1889 Margaret Aylward died.

Over the years an uneasy truce existed between the Coombe Ragged School and St Brigid's, with reports of occasional outbursts of intimidation on both sides. As time went on funds to the ragged school began to decline and there was also a decrease in the number of pupils. Other institutions and homes were providing destitute Catholic children with shelter and food, and there was less need for them to go to the proselytisers. Clashes between the two Coombe schools would occur now and again if the pupils happened to meet, with the Catholics taking the initiative and singing the jingle:

> Souper, souper on the wall,
> A half a loaf will do you all,
> A farthing candle to show you light,
> To read your Bible on a Friday night.

The reply would come back:

> Catholic, Catholic go to Mass,
> Ridin' on a big jack ass.

According to the Irish Church Missions Year Book for 1931 the 'souper' jingle was a vulgar doggerel poem which originated from the fact that some people were so afraid of being seen at their meetings that on a small table at which sat a teacher, were two candles and a Bible, the rest of the room being in darkness.

During my own school days the numbers attending the ragged school had dwindled considerably, but the hostile attitudes and superstitions which had begun in its early days continued to manifest themselves. I passed the school every day on my way down to St Brigid's, and one morning the gate, which was just at the corner of Newmarket Street, was wide open and I poked my head in to see what was inside. A short path led up to some steps at the top of which was a door. Frances Sheridan, my friend from Coombe Street, gave me a hefty push, which sent me right into the grounds as she screamed at the top of her voice, 'Don't go in there. They'll grab ye and drag ye into a room and make ye spit at a statue of the Blessed Virgin.' With that the door at the top of the steps opened and a figure appeared which put the fear of God into me and I never ran as quick in my life. I asked granny about this story when I got home but she laughed and told me it was all nonsense and she then told me of all the trouble there had been when the ragged school had first come to the Coombe.

In all my years passing it by I only saw the children about six times and they were always boys. They wore grey worsted suits and heavy black boots and their hair was shaved except for a bit in the front, but this hair style was quite common then with boys. All the boys, no matter how tall, wore short trousers. Some children from my school still jeered them as they marched out from their school in twos, their grey institutional garb setting them apart from other children, branding them as outcasts, and dependent on charity. In 1944 the ragged school closed down and the remaining children moved out to Boley, a large house which was once the home of Sir Valentine Grace, in Monkstown. The building on the Coombe was taken over by the Belfast Linen Company and in time suffered the same fate as many other historic buildings in the area. On its site now stands the new Corporation houses which were officially opened in 1980.

St. Nicholas of Myra, Francis Street

Pimlico — 1870s

Pimlico in 1870 was an untidy, desolate, decaying street. From the top of the Coombe at Ardee Street to Thomas Court Bawn (this includes Tripoli) there were thirty-five tenement houses, one dairy, two grocers, a spirit store, an operative distiller, a millwright, engineering and iron foundry, several yards which housed cows, pigs and horses, ruined buildings and waste ground.

Over the years small industries and various tradespeople seemed to come and go. The whole area around Pimlico and Tripoli — the Coombe, Marrowbone Lane and Cork Street — was also in a sad state of decline, yet at the beginning of the century manufacturers of cotton, linen and starch and many tradesmen lived in the numerous streets and alleys, and even in 1842 many of them were still there.

In 1871 Mr Doherty the brushmaker and Mr Hutchinson the brass finisher opened up in Nos 18 and 24 Pimlico. The following year Fry and Fielding the poplin manufacturers arrived and in 1876 Peter Cahill opened his stores, kiln and yard in No 37.

In 1878, however, most of the tenements in Pimlico were empty. From Nos 7 to 25 all the houses and yards and Mr Doherty the brushmaker were gone. The tenements on the Bawn side of Tripoli were still standing and were occupied, but some of them were in a very dangerous condition.

The overcrowding, the absence of proper sanitation, the increasing unemployment and resultant poverty, led to outbreaks of fever and epidemics of cholera, typhus, typhoid, croup, diphtheria and other diseases. Considering the unhealthy atmosphere and unhygienic surroundings it's a wonder any of the children survived.

There were no lavatories, so slop buckets had to be kept under the beds and these were then emptied into the cesspools in the back yards, and that only when they were full. Ash bins were also kept in the back yards and were not large enough to hold the amount of garbage from all the families. There was no proper or regular collection of rubbish or ash, so the spillage was all over the place. Flies and insects of every hue, shape and size and other vermin swarmed and scuttled about among the filthy, carrying disease and making the lives of the tenants an utter misery.

The vitality of the people was lowered by insufficient nourishment, exposure to the cold in badly heated rooms and the want of warm clothing. The death rate among them was quite high. They were forced to live in these conditions because there was simply nowhere else to live. However, Sir Charles Cameron, in his *Brief History of Public Health Administration in Dublin* wrote: 'The want of cleanliness, so often noticed in the case of the lower classes, is a factor in lowering their vital powers and rendering them more susceptible to infection.'

To add to their difficulties, there were no proper washing facilities and the great-granny and her neighbours had to do their washing on the banks of the Poddle which ran down Marrowbone Lane and turned into Tripoli and Pimlico before it turned left down the Coombe. The place where they did their washing was always known, even in my time, as the Banks of Pimlico.

Then rumours began to circulate and there was great talk of the old houses being knocked down and new ones being built. Many of the family's friends down in Pimlico had been forced to leave their rooms and the family watched with great interest the demolition of the street and wondered when their turn for eviction would come. The question didn't arise until nearly a hundred years later.

Pimlico began to take on a new face. Under the provisions of the Artisans' and Labourers' Act of 1875 the Corporation was given powers to compulsorily purchase land for the erection of artisans' dwellings. An area of four and a half acres on the Coombe and in Pimlico was cleared at a cost to the Corporation of nearly £20,000 and this land was then handed over to the Artisans' Dwellings Company for development.

This company had been formed in 1876 with the object of providing decent housing accommodation for the artisans of the city as well as to make profit for the company. When speaking at the laying of the foundation stone in the Coombe in 1880, Mr Richard Martin, the vice-chairman of the company, revealed the dual purpose of the directors when he said:

> It is the spirit of philanthropy which has actuated many of our shareholders and while this view will always largely pervade the actions of the directors, they thoroughly concur in the opinion expressed by the authoress of 'Homes of the London Poor', that this work must be carried out on thoroughly sound commercial principals and not as a charitable undertaking.

Artisan dwellings, Reginald Street, leading to Meath Place

According to Mr Martin, the proportion of children under the age of five years living in the Liberties at this time was double the proportion of the same age living in the rest of Dublin:

> In other words, while Dublin has 10 children under 5 years out of every 100, we have in our dwellings 20 children under 5 years out of every 100. At a recent Royal Sanitary Commission of Inquiry it was sworn in evidence, uncontradicted, and dwelt upon in the Report, that 100,000 of the inhabitants of this city were living in abodes unfit for human habitation.

When the family saw the nice, neat, red-brick houses and cottages mushrooming around, hopes were high that one of them might be acquired. But this was not to be so. Six houses on the north-west side of Tripoli were left standing and ours was one of them. Apparently the leases on them hadn't run out and they were considered to be sound enough to last for some time to come.

But even if the family's tenement had been demolished, we still wouldn't have got one of the new Artisans' Dwellings because tenants were required to produce two references of good moral character, to be in steady employment and not to indulge in drink. Whatever about great-grandad's moral character being beyond reproach, his employment was anything but steady and he drank like a fish. The two references would come from an employer and a clergyman, but great-grandad Coyne had a horse and cart and delivered coal and couldn't recommend himself.

The lucky artisans were usually men who had served in the British forces, Guinness workers, Jacob's employees, tradesmen or workers from the many distillers, breweries, and malt-houses which abounded in the area.

The main driving force behind the development in Pimlico and the Coombe was Lady Mary Jane Brabazon, wife of Reginald, who was the son of the eleventh Earl of Meath. She was the only surviving daughter of Admiral Sir Thomas Maitland, eleventh Earl of Lauderdale.

It was Lady Brabazon and Lord Ardilaun who largely financed the Dublin Artisans' Dwellings Company. She also financed the London Artisans' Company and during her lifetime she covered her husband's Dublin city property with excellent workingmens' dwellings, which were considered in many European countries to be an advanced type of housing for the 'lower classes'. She also initiated the setting up of many charitable institutions and organisations, both here and in England, and collaborated with her husband in the production of two books, *Social Aims* and *Thoughts on Imperial and Social Subjects*.

It would be true to say that without the concern shown by Lady Brabazon in improving the housing of the people in the Liberties at this time nothing would have been done. She undoubtedly spurred Lord Reginald into action. His explanation for the appalling housing conditions on his father's property was delivered in a speech to the Artisans' Dwellings Company meeting in 1883 when he outlined the problems which his father, Lord Meath, had faced in relation to improving his property earlier:

> Very few could understand the difficulties which surround the tenure of property in towns and the tenure of property in land. With regard to the property under notice his ancestors had leased a great portion of it away for ever, and other portions had been leased for periods which were practically in perpetuity, and it was only in isolated bits, here and there, that the landlord had control over his property.

The residents of the slums certainly didn't understand the earl's problems any more than he understood theirs. As far as they were concerned, he owned the land; they also thought he owned all the houses, and therefore he was responsible for the condition of the tenements.

When eventually the Artisans' Dwellings were built in the Liberties the people said it was about time that the earl called a halt to the rot, or at least to some of it, because there were still many tenements and hovels left.

The foundation stone was laid on 20 December 1880. Lady Brabazon recalls in her diaries that it was a lovely day for the ceremony. There was a large gathering of notabilities, including the lord lieutenant and Lady Cowper, and the lord mayor, Mr Grey. He was the owner of *The Freeman's Journal* and Lady Brabazon describes him as a Land Leaguer. He was accompanied by his secretary and an escort of the Metropolitan Police, as well as a force of police of the local A Division in charge of Superintendent Byrne.

Accompanying the lord lieutenant and Countess Cowper was Lord William Compton, His Excellency's private secretary and aide de camp. There was also a guard of honour of the Coldstream Guards, and to add an air of festivity to the occasion, music was supplied by the Regimental Fife and Drum Band.

With all this razzle-dazzle, one would have expected a great turn-out of locals to witness the event. But Lady Brabazon writes, 'Very few people were about and among the populace there didn't seem to be much enthusiasm.'

This was a time of great political activity in the country. The Land League had been formed the year before and 'the land for the people' became the slogan of rural Ireland. In the Liberties there were many Fenian and Land League supporters. Many of the people living in the area had come, like my mother's people, from rural areas in the aftermath of the Famine in 1848. They had suffered hunger and eviction before settling in the Liberties and bad memories die hard.

Landlords were treated with odium and Lord Meath was no exception. In her diaries Lady Brabazon records in relation to Lord Brabazon, 'They even threatened his life on Christmas Day. So much for gratitude among the easily led Irish.' The reference here is to the Land Leaguers in Wicklow, where the Earl of Meath resided and had property.

Pimlico — 1880s

Within two years the houses were completed. The entire area was bounded on the south by the Upper Coombe, on the west by Pimlico, on the north by Cole Alley and on the east by Meath Street. Two main thoroughfares at right angles, forty feet wide, extended from Cole Alley to the Coombe and from Meath Street to Pimlico.

However, it wasn't until 1885 that the sixteen houses and twelve cottages on the south side of Tripoli and a short distance on the west side of Pimlico were completed. The widening of the roadway in Tripoli was undertaken at this time, which increased the width of Tripoli from twenty-eight to forty feet.

It was hoped that the new houses would not only bring improvement in the health, morals and condition of the people but that they would increase their working power and decrease pauperism, crime and disease and so save the ratepayers a lot of money.

In the centre of the thoroughfares an ornamental fountain was erected with a cattle trough attached:

> The structure, which is of cast iron, is of monumental proportions being fully 18 feet high by 12 feet diameter and it is set on a platform of masonry. It consists of a central fountain with amp pillars surmounted by a dome of highly carved tracery supported on eight columns. The drinking fountain in the centre has four basins with marsh marigold beautifully carved on them and from the arms above each basin are suspended drinking cups convenient to the hand. The pedestal on which the basins are fixed is also finely modelled, the part below being enriched with water lilies, while the four sides of the pedestal above show representations in relief emblematic of an island lake with swans and storks. The columns which support the dome are set octagonally, and on them rest cusped arches above which rise shield panels; griffins guard the eight corners and behind these rise the dome of ornamental tracery. The whole is finely finished in every detail and richly painted in marone colour and gold. The work is the production of Messrs MacFarlane and Co. Ironfounders, Glasgow, and the cost has been defrayed by joint contributions of the Artisans' Dwellings Co., the Municipal Council and the Fountains Committee of the City.

The site contained two-storey houses in front and one-storey cottages behind in open squares. Every house and cottage had its own supply of water direct from the mains and each had its own back yard and water closet.

Altogether the company built 210 dwellings containing 594 rooms. One-storey cottages cost three shillings and sixpence a week rent, three-roomed houses cost five and sixpence and four-roomed two-storey houses cost six and six and seven and six a week. These rents were considered quite high at the time and could only be afforded by people with regular employment.

Before the clearance the population in the area had been 984 and it now rose to 1100. The Corporation received a head rent of £200 per annum from the Artisans' Dwellings Company. The expenditure by the company on the construction of the dwellings was over £26,000 and they provided an additional £600 per annum in rates to the Corporation.

Lord and Lady Brabazon established a fund to give prizes to the tenants who kept their houses in the neatest and most orderly way. These prizes were offered annually for the best kept houses and cottages and also for window-gardening. Speaking at the third annual

Reginald, 12th Earl of Meath

distribution of prizes in the Antient Concert Rooms, Great Brunswick Street (now Pearse Street) on Friday 2 March 1883, Dr Grimshaw, the registrar general, gave a description of the ritual which had to be gone through before winners were selected:

> Deciding on the prizewinners wasn't an easy matter. The tenants had to go through a rigorous test which involved many visits over a long period by a panel of judges. The judges acted in pairs having agreed to inspect and report upon certain groups of buildings. They held about 20 meetings and paid upwards of 4000 visits exclusive of any abortive visits when, owing to the illness or absence from home of the occupiers, the judges had to call again.
>
> The number of competitors in 1882 was 145 against 106 in 1881, the number of tenants being 353 and 263 respectively. Thus the competitors were 41.9% of the tenants in 1882 against 40.3% in 1881, showing a slight but gratifying increase in the desire to compete.
>
> No rigid rule was laid down in the number of visits to be paid to the house of each competitor. Some were visited only twice, others three, four and five times, and occasionally even six times during the year.
>
> When valid reasons were given for defects noticed, other visits were made to give the candidates a fair chance. Allowances were made for sickness or sudden loss of employment of the breadwinner. An effort was made to visit each tenant at different periods of the day, affording the judges opportunity of testing the energy and care with which the mistress of the house regulated her establishment.
>
> In grouping the tenants for competition care was taken to place, as far as possible, in the same group those who could compete upon equal terms with one another. When the final decision came to be made the competition was so close that the judges had to pay repeated visits in several instances, more to look for defects to determine differences than to search for particular merits. In some cases the perfection of cleanliness and tidiness seemed to have been attained.
>
> On the whole, although the proportion of competitors is but slightly above that of 1881, the competition has been much closer. In addition to the prizewinners, the judges deem it right to state that a considerable number of the competitors have so closely approached the winning numbers, that with the consent of Lord and Lady Brabazon, they wish to state that they have arranged those tenants in a command list, in consideration of the admirable efforts which they have made to keep their houses neat and cleanly during the year.

Lady Brabazon was high in her praise for the housewives who had proved themselves worthy of prizes by being neat and clean and well advised:

> My friends, first I must congratulate you — the wives of the tenants of the Dublin Artisans' Dwellings Company — on your success. I address those remarks more especially to you because as a woman it is more becoming in me to speak to those of my own sex and also because if a dwelling has been found to be clean and comfortable, depend upon it, a woman's hand has had the doing of it. The prizes to be distributed today are not to consist of money only.
>
> Lord Brabazon and I thought it would be more acceptable to you to receive more lasting tokens of success to adorn the homes of which you have taken such good care. The winners of the first prizes will therefore receive a present in addition to the money prize, whilst all successful competitors will have a printed certificate to hang up in their homes.

Lady Mary Jane Brabazon, the driving force behind the Artisans' Dwellings Company.

You are aware that the prizes are given for neatness and cleanliness and for window-gardening, but perhaps you are not equally cognisant of the fact that the prizes are, indirectly, rewards for temperance and no prize can be given in a cottage where a person of intemperate habits resides. In some cases this rule may seem hard, and yet on the whole, I trust it may commend itself to you, for as long as intemperance continues to be so frightfully prevalent, it is clearly the duty of those who see the evil of it to endeavour to arrest its progress and to foster habits of temperance.

Wholesome dwellings with plenty of good water and air and, let me add, the absence of dirt, are a step in that direction.

The success of the temperance movement would be assured if all women would support it. Women could make their homes so attractive that drinking-bars shall be deserted. It is on women that devolves the great responsibilities of bringing up children, forming their habits and moulding their opinions.

Happily, a good many women are already strong supporters of this movement and doing their best to advance its interest. There is one right of which women may well be proud and which has been generally conceded to them — namely, that wherever misery and suffering prevail it is theirs to be first and foremost in relieving it. I venture to express the opinion that it would be worthy of the nobler part of woman's nature, if, instead of adding as we sometimes do, by ignorance or by prejudice, to religious or political differences, we oftener tried to soften them down. If we tried to persuade husbands or brothers that however much others may differ from us, yet when there is good proof to the contrary, we have no right to conclude that our neighbour may not be actuated by good motives.

Providence has decreed that an equal amount of wealth is not given to all. The rich cannot do without the poor and it has yet to be proved that the poor can do without the rich. I will conclude by wishing you from my heart that on those new houses which have been lately erected for your benefit, heaven's blessing may rest and that health and happiness may be bestowed upon you and all those that are dear to you.

The Recorder of Dublin added his admonition to the worthy women when he said, as reported in the *Evening Mail:*

The first thing to be done was to make the houses of the people habitable, then men would stay at home with their wives and children and the women would become centres of order, both for their own homes and for the surrounding district.

There had been a moral resurrection in the Coombe District and Liberties generally and it would scarcely be recognised now by those who had known it in olden times.

In the reign of Henry VIII, the district was first given as a grant to the members of the Meath and Brabazon family. At the time it was one of the fairest and finest portions of the city of Dublin. It subsequently decayed very much and he could very well understand the interest that the Meath and Brabazon family now took in endeavouring to improve it, and if not to bring it back to its former condition of prosperity, at least to do all that they could possibly do to alleviate and ameliorate the condition of those residing in it.

There was poetic justice as well as historic propriety in the great work that they were engaged in. Lady Brabazon had spoken of the miserable habits of drunkeness, the miserable results of which did not stop with the children or the wives of the drunkard. As a matter of fact, he could state that 95% of the ordinary crime of the city was due to the misery of the homes of the people and that misery was due to their love of intoxicating liquor, their desire for intoxicating drinks being due to the misery of their homes.

Visiting Royalty

On Thursday 9 April 1885 there was great excitement in Pimlico and in the surrounding streets. It began suddenly around midday and like a bush fire the air of excitement blazed through the streets, squares, lanes, alleys, courts and into the tenement hall. Door knockers bang-banged, knuckles rattled on windows, and up the tenements the news was bellowed: 'The Prince of Wales is in Reginald Street. Quick, hurry you'll miss him. The world and Garrett Reilly is down there. He's givin' out money.'

Nobody really believed it but still everything was dropped — including children. Curiosity and the promise of a bit of excitement, not to mention the idea of a handout, enticed the neighbours down in droves. Anyway, it wasn't every day of the week that members of the Royal Family dropped in to pay their respects.

Meath Street, Gray Street and Reginald Street were black with people all trying to get a dekko of the prince. Some of them had no manners at all and were singing:

> The Prince of Wales is gone to jail, parley vu,
> The Prince of Wales is gone to jail, parley vu,
> The Prince of Wales is gone to jail,
> For riding an ass without a tail,
> With your inkey, stinkey, parley vu.

In the beginning all the action was in Reginald Square, outside the home of Mrs Coady, which was No 18. Her lovely cottage had been picked specially for the royal viewing because earlier in the year, on 23 January, Mrs Coady had won first prize in the annual competition for the cleanest and neatest house and also got the first prize for window-gardening. All in all she got £3 and a framed certificate to adorn her wall.

So Mrs Coady was out of her mind with delight at the honour of having the prince call upon her. She brought him in and he gave the cottage a good look over and she told him her husband had a marvellous job as a drayman in Guinness's Brewery earning a pound a week and out of that four shillings a week went on the rent. His Royal Highness remarked that the construction of the cottage seemed to be of a very durable character; then he went out the back yard and had a look at the outside WC and expressed his approval of the sanitary arrangements.

He was so impressed by the cleanliness that he requested that he might see the other side of the picture and be shown as dirty a house as possible. The surprised chairman of the Artisans' Dwellings Company said that the best substitute that could be thought of was a house with a 'temporary' goat in it.

The company rules stated categorically that animals couldn't be kept, but this goat had a special licence to be milked on the premises. This was the nearest the prince could get to a dirty house. The owner of the goat had been the recipient of a prize the previous year, prior to the acquisition of the nanny, whose 'currants' were the only evidence of dirt which could be found for the prince.

His Royal Highness then proceeded to Brabazon Square where he dropped into No 14, a three-bedroomed cottage, before continuing into Pimlico. Altogether he spent forty minutes in the area, and when he got back to his carriage several requests were made to shake his hand which he graciously compiled with, and a number of not over-clean hands were thrust through the window of the royal carriage.

One enthusiastic woman exclaimed on the departure of the prince, 'Glory be to God, he's been in Elbow Lane anyhow,' Elbow Lane being the name of the filthy alley which formerly stood on what is now Gray Street.

Accompanying the Prince of Wales on his rounds was his son, Prince Albert Victor, the Duke of Clarence. He was a sorry looking sight in a coat several sizes too big for him and his appearance was the cause of much merriment and comment. The reason for his odd attire was later explained. Before the royal entourage arrived in Reginald Square it had paid a brief visit to the slums of Golden Lane. Just as the royal visitors were about to dismount from the carriage, a bucket of slop was discharged into the channel by a woman from one of the large tenements and the unfortunate young Prince Albert slipped and fell down into the stinking contents. All the newspaper reports described it as cabbage water but the local wags, who could always be relied upon to embellish every unfortunate incident, insisted that it was a more obnoxious substance, and that, furthermore, the woman had done it on purpose. Be that as it may, the young prince sustained no injury, only a certain loss of face and his father is reported to have said that it would do him good. After a wipe-down with handkerchiefs, Sir Dighton Probyn, a man of enormous proportions, took off his top-coat and put it around the Prince's shoulders. This helped to smother the worst of the smell and cover the unsightly stains on the prince's clothes.

Sir Charles Cameron, Superintendent Medical Officer of Health, must have been up the wall because he was the cause of the royal visit to the locality in the first place. The Prince of Wales was in Dublin attending a meeting of the Royal Commission relating to the dwellings of the working classes of which His Royal Highness was chairman. That was his story, but Parnell didn't believe a word of it. However, Sir Charles proposed that since the Prince was here to discuss the housing of the lower classes, he might as well take a trip into some of these areas and see some of the wretched dwellings in which the poor lived, as well as some of the model dwellings which the Artisans' Dwellings Company had built.

The proposal met with some opposition from the prince's entourage, but ultimately it was agreed that he should visit the slums, but strictly incognito, because it was believed in some quarters that the prince's life would not be safe in Dublin's purlieu.

There were, of course, good grounds for these fears as the country was in a state of high political excitement and an election was imminent. Parnell and the Land League objected most strongly to the prince's presence in Ireland. The former referred to it as an electioneering stunt and accused the two English political parties in Ireland of using the royal personage for the purpose of injuring and insulting the Irish Nationalist Party and of impeding, if possible, their work.

While Sir Charles Cameron believed that the poorer classes in Dublin had generous instincts and would respect any visitor with kind intentions who came among them, Parnell believed that the people would not allow their hospitable nature and cordial disposition to carry them into any attitude which might be taken as one of condoning the past or satisfaction with the present state of affairs.

All the Conservative papers made great political capital out of the visit, saying that it showed how loyal the Irish people were and how content under present political conditions, and the London *Times* stated that the prince's sortie into the slums was of great importance.

The areas to which the prince had been taken were carefully chosen, as the residents were ex-British soldiers and employees of firms whose allegiances were to the British crown and empire. The reception they gave the prince was not a true indication of how the majority of

The Prince of
Wales in the
Liberties in 1885

the Dublin people felt, because many, including my own family, wouldn't and didn't welcome his presence.

On Friday 19 September 1890 Her Majesty, Pauline Elizabeth Ottolie Louise of Roumania, daughter of Prince Hermann of Weid, and well known by her *nom de plume* of 'Carmen Sylva', arrived in Kingstown. The royal party then proceeded to Bray, where it was intended that the band of the King's Royal Rifles should be to greet the queen and to play the Roumanian national anthem, but unfortunately, either by accident or design, the bandsmen got onto the wrong train and arrived too late for the event. Rumour had it, of course, that the mistake was deliberate just to cause confusion.

The queen was here at the invitation of the Earl of Meath and was expected to spend three weeks among the people of Bray. Some members of Bray County Council made a big thing of the fact that the earl hadn't fixed her up at his own residence in Killruddery. Instead, the royal guest was accommodated at No 3 Royal Marine Terrace, the home of Mrs Breslin, which was a beautifully situated hotel. It commanded a splendid view of the sea, with the hills of Killiney on the one hand and Bray on the other, and the fine esplanade in front of the window. The tranquil surroundings were expected to give Her Majesty an opportunity to study types of Irish life which might find a place in the next literary work of the gifted queen.

One the day after her arrival the queen was taken on a tour of Dublin by the Earl of Meath, and was met by the lord mayor and his wife. The queen had specially requested to see the poorer parts of Dublin, so after a jaunt around Merrion Square and Stephen's Green, the royal entourage swung into York Street and in no time at all arrived in the Coombe.

The earl was very proud of his Liberties, particularly the Artisans' Dwellings, as well he might be. On this lovely Saturday afternoon in autumn they looked their best, with their warm red-brick frontage, the flowers in full bloom in the window-boxes, the ornamental fountain an eyecatching central focal point and the green shrubs decorating each corner of the crossroads of Reginald Street and Gray Street.

The procession of carriages accompanying the royal visitor attracted a great deal of attention. A large crowd had gathered in Gray Street and, as it was a Saturday afternoon, the area of Meath Street and the Coombe was a hive of activity with shoppers, children, and countrymen with cartloads of vegetables and turf.

Some of the residents had got wind of the word that the queen was visiting, but most of the onlookers hadn't a clue what was going on. My granny was one of them. She was returning home with the shopping and was tripping it down Meath Street pushing a high-wheeled perambulator, which was occupied by my mother, then two years old, when she heard all the commotion. Instead of turning into Cole Alley (Meath Place), she followed the crowd rushing down to see the ruggy-up in Gray Street.

The shopping was sharing the perambulator with my mother, except for a pig's head, which was dripping with brine and was wrapped in a piece of paper tucked under my granny's oxter. The crowd began to mill around, pushing and shoving and granny was finding it hard to negotiate the pram. Suddenly, the pig's head slipped out from under her arm and between the jigs and reels it disappeared underfoot. Her cries of 'Where's me pig's head?' could be heard all over Gray Street and were misinterpreted by some loyal residents to mean that she was calling the queen of Roumania 'pig's head'. She never found the pig's head and barely got away without losing her life. Her reception at home when she confessed her loss and how it came about through rushing to get a look at royalty caused her never to forget the visit of the Queen of Roumania.

The royal procession didn't halt for too long and Her Majesty didn't get out to meet the people. One woman was the delighted recipient of a bunch of flowers which the queen handed out to her through the window of her carriage. The procession then headed off towards Thomas Street to Christchurch Cathedral, where Her Majesty inspected the cathedral.

The novel which the Queen was writing at the time was named *Eileen Vaughan* or *The Paths of Peril,* was set in the British Isles and was to appear the following spring.

The Prince of Wales outside Mrs Coady's cottage, 18 Reginald Square, 1885

Mrs Coady anxiously awaiting the Prince Consort's pleasure.

MRS. COADY'S COTTAGE, DUBLIN—EXTERIOR

MRS. COADY'S COTTAGE, DUBLIN—INTERIOR

Pimlico Playground

On the day on which the foundation stone for the Artisans' Dwellings was being laid in the Coombe area, Lady Brabazon put her eye on a piece of land just at the corner of Cole Alley and Pimlico and the thought came to her mind that here was a nice spot on which to provide an open space for the people of the area. So she immediately got in touch with her father-in-law, Lord Meath, seeking his permission to develop the site. In her diaries, the countess described the particular spot she had in mind as 'a wretched place now, with ruins where cows and pigs are kept, and Reginald and I think we might make it into a nice garden or playground with a Coffee House at the corner. Such is our Chateau-en-Espagne.'

And so the idea for what was later to become the Pimlico Playground or as it was called locally, The Swingin' Boats, was conceived, but it took seven years before it became a reality, on 3 September 1887.

The opening of the playground took place two months before my granny got married. She was twenty-six years old and the two events were always linked together in her mind. The Earl of Meath also had occasion to remember the event personally for two days before the opening he took his seat in the House of Commons for the first time.

It was a Saturday afternoon and the weather was very showery but it didn't dampen the spirits of the large crowd which had gathered for the opening ceremony. Pimlico and Tripoli were elaborately decorated for the occasion with bunting and flags stretched across the street and banners and Union Jacks flying from poles sticking out from the windows. A large dais had been erected in the playground, and drawn up in front of this was the band of the Black Watch playing a selection of airs for the entertainment of all.

The whole area was thronged with people, police and soldiers, long before the arrival of the dignitaries. There was an air of great excitement — children were everywhere, for after all, this splendid occasion was for them. Everyone was singing and dancing to the music and those who lived near the playground were hanging out through the open windows of the Artisans' Dwellings and the tenements.

The band took the crowd on a 'Musical Tour of Europe' by Coaradi; then they all danced to the valse 'A Toi' by Waldteufel, and to 'My Lost Love' by Marie Dupres, and sang with great verve to a selection from 'The Bohemian Girl' by Balfe. Then followed the grand march 'Festival' by F. N. Lohr, 'Lucia di Lammermoor' by Donizetti, and 'L'Oiseau Dols' by Le Thiere.

While all this carousing was going on among the common people in Pimlico, another important event was taking place up in New Row South, off the other end of the Coombe. Lady Brabazon wasn't content with doing things by half measure, so instead of giving the children of the Liberties one playground she gave us two. The smaller of the two was in New Row and this she officially opened first, with an equal amount of pomp and ceremony.

The entourage then set off for Pimlico. It consisted of the lord lieutenant and the Marchioness of Londonderry, the Duke of Leinster, Archbishop Walsh, the recorder of Dublin, Lord Ardilaun, Sir Richard Martin, Venerable Archbishop Mahon PP, Mr Spencer, William Moore the physician ordinary to the queen in Ireland, and a host of other dignitaries, along with Lord and Lady Meath and their family.

Ireland's first Playground, Pimlico, opened in 1887

The Liberties was always a community of mixed religions and political affiliations, as well as mixed nationalities. Centuries of living and working together gave rise to a fair amount of inter-marriage which complicated allegiances within families. Some Catholics were very pro-British and had served in the British Army, while some Protestants were very anti-British and either had sympathy with or were actively involved in the fight for Home Rule or supported the Fenians' ideals of an independent Irish state with absolutely no connections with Britain. Then there were the Catholics, like my own family, who were very Fenian and anti-British but were also very critical of the Catholic clergy and their denunciation of the Fenians. So all in all there was a great mix, but none of the complications mattered when there was a bit of fun to be had and it all made for interesting relationships.

So everyone turned out to enjoy themselves, whether to cheer or to jeer. Meath Place, which had formerly been called Cole Alley, was thronged to capacity. The carriages containing the earl's party couldn't get next, near nor towards the playground entrance, until, after much pushing and shoving, the police finally made a path through the crowd. Amid boos, cheers and hisses, the party were eventually conducted to the dais and the band of the Black Watch struck up the British national anthem. This was greeted with more hisses and whistles.

The Earl of Meath then stepped forward and welcomed all present. He said that 'Notwithstanding that Dublin possessed one of the largest parks in the world there was more or less necessity for such playgrounds as the one they were now opening.' He believed that there was only one park in the world bigger than the Phoenix Park and that was the one in Philadelphia. But the Phoenix Park was practically of little use to the children of the poor people living in such districts as the Liberties. It was too far from these people, and they could not afford the time or the money that was required to get them to the Phoenix Park.

There was one among them, who, he thought, had done more than any other private individual in the way of providing open spaces. He referred to Lord Ardilaun (hear hear). The park which Lord Ardilaun had given to the people of Dublin was one of the prettiest and most beautifully laid out in the world. He, Lord Meath, had passed that day through Stephen's Green and the manner in which it was laid out reflected the greatest credit (hear hear). Besides they had not been idle in Dublin with regard to open spaces. Some time ago a fund had been raised for the purpose of providing employment in a period of distress and a large sum of money had been collected, with which the grounds of Christchurch Cathedral and St Mary's Church were laid out. These grounds were not yet open to the public, the reason being that the Corporation of Dublin did not possess the powers which the municipal authorities possessed in London with regard to open spaces. However, under an Act passed this session the Corporation of Dublin now had these necessary powers and he hoped they would lose no time in availing themselves of these powers under the Act for the benefit of the poor and working classes.

His Excellency the lord lieutenant said that he had great pleasure in declaring the Pimlico Playground open. He thanked those present for the cordial reception they had given Lady Londonderry and himself. He concurred that such open spaces were greatly required by the people of Dublin and he concurred with Lady Meath about the absolute necessity of playgrounds for the children of the working classes in this city. It was a matter which had been overlooked. He hoped that the good results which had followed the opening of such playgrounds in England would follow the opening of the two playgrounds provided by the Earl of Meath, which were the first of their kind not only in the metropolis but in Ireland. He was sure he was expressing the feelings of the people of Dublin when he said that they felt great gratitude for the generous impulse which prompted Lord Meath in providing these playgrounds.

With that the heavens opened and amid cheers and hisses from the crowd the proceedings were terminated and everyone had to run for cover into the tenement houses and up the Long Entry.

Next day, Sunday, hundreds of children from near and far descended upon Pimlico and there was only holy open desolation as they congregated outside the gates waiting for the playground to open. There were two separate play areas, the right-hand side was for boys and the left-hand side for girls. This segregation remained in force for as long as the playground was there. There were no objections to this from any quarter, and in fact everyone regarded it as only right and proper. The children didn't mind because they all knew that rules were made to be broken and so there was endless fun crossing over into forbidden territory with the excitement of subterfuge and capture thrown in for good measure.

In the beginning the playground was well provided for with all kinds of apparatus, particularly the boys' side. Here there was a skittle-alley, fly-pole, a springboard or high jump, see-saws and horizontal bars. The fly-pole was a huge wooden pole, like a maypole, with very strong, thick ropes attached at the top. The idea was to grab a rope, give a good run with giant strides and jump onto the enormous knots at the end. It was great fun, but in the interest of propriety it was forbidden to the girls. Being caught in the act meant instant expulsion from the playground and repreated transgression carried a barring order. The girls' side lacked the wildly exciting apparatus of the boys' — they only had swings, see-saws, boats and horizontal bars.

The playground opened every day, including Sunday, but after a time the Sunday opening was discontinued. It was maintained by the Earl of Meath at a sum of £100 per annum, but as time went on the upkeep increased and after thirty-five years the earl got fed up paying and he wrote to the Corporation that, owing to financial pressure, he was compelled to close the playground.

The future of the playground was now threatened. The high cost of replacing broken and worn-out apparatus wasn't the only reason. The person whose brain-child the playground was, Lady Meath, had died four years earlier, and there was no one now to care about the children of the Liberties or their playground.

In 1921 the earl's agent informed the Corporation of the earl's intention and it was suggested that the Corporation might purchase the ground from Lord Meath with a view either to developing the site as building ground or to reopening it as a playground. In the former event a long lease would be given at a rent of £50 per annum, or in the latter case at a rent of £35 per annum, as long as it should be maintained by the Corporation as a free public playground for the children. The Corporation gave the matter careful consideration, but came to the conclusion that, while it was very desirable that it should be reopened, the cost of maintenance, if taken over by the Corporation, would place too great a burden on the rate-payers. The Corporation then proposed that if Lord Meath would undertake to maintain the playground as heretofore, it would recommend the Council to contribute a sum of £135 annually, which sum would consist of £100 for upkeep, plus the yearly rent of £35.

The upshot of all this was that Lord Ardee, acting for his father, agreed to keep the playground open on these conditions. And so, at the beginning of 1922, the gates of the Swingin' Boats swung open once more to the great delight of the children in Pimlico.

With each generation of children born in the Liberties, the playground was the centre of the outdoor activities. It also attracted children from other areas and became the scene for gang warfare between the children from Pimlico, who believed that the playground was rightfully theirs, and the children from Francis Street, Oliver Bond Flats and Maryland.

In the 1930s, when I was growing up, the caretaker was a Mr McGowan, an old white-haired man who lived by the Tenters. He was extremely cranky and was never called anything but 'oul' McGowan'. He expended most of his energy during his hours of work in chasing us out of the playground for the slightest misdemeanour. For this reason we delighted in tormenting him and in turn he thought nothing of giving us a belt of a stick if he got near enough. At a safe distance we would chant:

> Oul' McGowan, the cock of the town
> One leg up and the other leg down.

During the second World War, the playground was again closed for some time, while underground air-raid shelters were being dug. We would never have been able to get into them if the occasion to do so had arisen because they were kept locked and the gate to the playground was also locked. From this time on the playground only opened intermittently, as oul' McGowan was getting on in years and he was finding it increasingly difficult to cope with the 'blackguards', as he called us.

The Corporation Compulsory Purchase Order of 1955 for Pimlico and Marrowbone Lane was the final blow to the first and oldest playground in Ireland, the one in New Row having been closed many years before.

Fountain on site of Manor Courthouse prior to its demolition in 1957

Housing

In 1897 a lot of trouble was brewing between the tenants of the Artisans' Dwellings and the company over the raising of the rents by threepence per week. New sanitary arrangements had been installed in the houses and the company was insisting that the tenants should pay. When they refused the company issued them with notices to quit. This gave rise to a tremendous amount of local agitation, meetings and demonstrations. The tenants were supported by Artisans' Dwellers in other parts of the city and by the United Labourers' Union, of which there were many members in the area.

Through the columns of the *Evening Herald* the working men of Dublin were invited to assemble and protest against the company's action on Friday 22 October 1897 in Gray's Square. The street was thronged with locals and workers from all over the city, and James Connolly addressed them on the evils of rack-renting landlords and exposed the profits which the company was making. A few days later another meeting in Rialto called for a common defence fund and for support, financial and otherwise, for the Coombe tenants in their gallant fight. Mr William Field MP spoke as did Mr Pat O'Brien MP, who appealed to the company to look back over the history of the Land War in Ireland saying:

> What Parnell [cheers] did for the tenant farmers his followers were prepared to do for the town tenants. If the Artisans' Dwellings Company did not take Mr Field's valuation, the fight will go on and they must be willing to take less, before the workingmen of Dublin would be done with them.'

On 3 November a meeting of the Dublin District Labour Council passed a resolution giving the tenants every support in the fight against the company.

One of the tenants, Michael McGuinness, from No 13 Brabazon Square, was brought before the courts for refusing to pay his rent, but his case was adjourned for a week. A few days later a number of tenants appeared before the recorder in Green Street Court. Mr T.M. Healy MP appeared for them, and it was agreed on his suggestion that the existing tenants should pay up all rents due and that the company should not raise the rents before 1 January 1899. The tenants and the company accepted this and the ejectment notices were withdrawn.

There was great rejoicing among the locals at the outcome, even among those living in the tenements who had been solidly behind their neighbours in the fight. If the evictions had taken place, they had been prepared to prevent anyone else from taking over the tenancies of the houses and a complete boycott of the company had been planned. It had been a marvellous demonstration of neighbourly support and co-operation.

The old court-house at the corner of our street was demolished that year (1898) also and in the following year, a memorial fountain was erected by the Earl of Meath to mark the site of the manor court. All the banging and pounding on our side wall nearly knocked our house down, and behind the wallpaper the hairy plaster could be heard crumbling and cracking. However, when the structure was complete it certainly did add greatly to the appearance of the Bawn. A description of the fountain in the daily papers was as follows:

> The design of the fountain, which was selected by the Earl of Meath, represents the Dolphin

in capture, and is executed in relief upon a table of white marble, the whole being enclosed by a framing of carved stone. The fountain is reached from the footpath by two granite steps. On either side, close up to the monument, is erected an ornamental railing set on a granite base, and within which are planted trees and shrubs, which add greatly to the appearance of the enclosure. The fountain is erected close up to the wall. The marble Dolphin was sculptured in Italy by Bellosic and it is a copy of a very ancient fountain to be found in Thun in Switzerland. The stone setting and design were executed by Mr James Beckett of Dublin. An inscription at the top reads 'This fountain erected in 1898 by the Earl and Countess of Meath, marks the site of the ancient Manor Court of the Earls of Meath.'

Fountain on site of Manor Courthouse and some local boys. Opening Ceremony 1898

The ceremony to open the fountain took place on the afternoon of Friday 20 May. The earl was unable to attend as he was indisposed and the countess was abroad for health reasons so Lady May Brabazon did the honours and presented the lord mayor, Mr David Tallon, with a beautifully framed photograph of the fountain. The usual dignitaries of church and state were present, but it was a more sombre affair on this occasion, which was probably due to the fact that Mr Gladstone had died the previous day and it might have been felt that any display of music and gaiety would have been inappropriate. The Rev F.W. Greer, Rector of St Catherine's Church in Thomas Street, gave an historical account of the site and the lord mayor sang the praises of the Earl and Countess of Meath, and on behalf of the local tenants he thanked them for the playground, the fountain and the Artisans' Dwellings. He also informed the gathering that the earl would rather spend one hour at home among his people than ten hours in the Palace of Westminster. The family and the neighbours were hanging out of the windows listening to all this, and they thought the last remark rather strange, since none of them had clapped eyes on the earl for one minute, never mind one hour, in the last eleven years.

During the whole month of September 1898, the *Daily Nation* newspaper carried out investigations into the conditions of life in the slums of Dublin. Every day the paper's commissioner visited the tenements, hovels, alleys and courts in which the people were forced to live and everywhere the story was the same, squalor, misery, and degradation, which had to be seen to be believed. Many of the houses visited and described were the same ones which had been reported as unfit for human habitation in 1871 by *The Freeman's Journal* and Dr Grimshaw. The tenements in School Street and Story's Villas in Taylor's Lane got particular mention, yet these houses were still inhabited in my own time. Ashe Street was 'rotten from end to end', and Nos 26, 27 and 28 Meath Place, three tenements sharing an enclosed passage at the rear, were totally disgusting and absolutely stinking. In 1894 Meath Place had two smallpox cases and in 1895 one case. The Artisans' Dwellings in Pimlico and Brabazon Square were singled out for praise 'with their open spaces and neatly arranged rows of houses'.

A clergyman who was interviewed by the *Daily Nation* commissioner had this to say about a particularly bad area, which showed how concerned he was for the people who *didn't* live there:

> If an epidemic were to break out in this parish it would work terrible havoc. The great majority of our people are fish dealers, and the fish they don't sell one day they leave in their rooms until the following morning, when they wash them under the nearest waterpipe and bring them out for sale, and in many cases succeed in disposing of them. I can remember a case where a party was attacked by Irish cholera and there was a large quantity of shell-fish placed by the bed, the shell-fish being intended for sale on the first opportunity. And these articles are not sold in the courts about us here. The people here are much too cute for that. But they are hawked around roads and squares and suburban districts in search of customers and much of this class of fish is disposed of in this way.

Although the Artisans' Dwellings had received honourable mention in the September *Daily Nation,* a short report had appeared in the *Irish Builder* on 15 July 1898 on the Gray Street Fountain, (built in 1881 at the same time as the Artisans's Dwellings), that was anything but complimentary. It described the ornamental iron lattice-work as more suitable for a garden than a fountain and said that as a fountain it had long since ceased to be of any benefit to the residents, that there was no water supply in it and that furthermore it was a useless ornament as well as being an unsightly obstruction. The fountain was only fifteen years old and had already fallen into decay. Thirty-one years later the residents and parishioners of St Catherine's in Meath Street subscribed to the erection of a statue to commemorate the centenary of Catholic Emancipation, in 1929, which took the place of the old fountain within the ornamental iron lattice-work.

My mother was ten years of age when the *Daily Nation* investigations took place. She had vivid memories of some of the conditions which existed at the time, particularly in relation to our own housing conditions. The cesspit which had been in the back yard was of such horror to her that even though it was well and truly banked up with earth in my time, I was forbidden to even walk near it. Her remembrance of her illness with typhoid fever and of the death of her brother Ned from typhoid was always present in her mind and she lived in fear of the spot.

In due course a lavatory was installed in each of the tenement houses, but because of the numbers of people in the houses, the lavatories in time became health hazards. When I was growing up, the door on our lavatory was about eighteen inches down from the top and the same distance up from the ground which gave anyone without a fine view of whoever was operating within and as there was no bolt on the door a body was in a very vulnerable position indeed. Our house was a small tenement compared with others in the street but even so the WC had to cater for about thirty people in my mother's time and roughly nineteen in my own time.

Because the hall doors were always open, every Tom, Dick and Harry came in off the street to use the 'inconvenience' as we called it. This meant that obeying the call of nature was fraught with danger for the tenants. It was for this reason that women were reluctant to use the lavatories and small children couldn't be let near them unaccompanied, especially at night, because the halls, stairways and yards were unlit. Their needs had to be met by the use of the slop-bucket under the bed, which the women always had to empty because men were too embarrassed, or so they said. Some poet, with a problem on his mind, wrote on the lavatory wall one day:

Here I sit in a funny caper
Came to shit and brought no paper,
Time is short and I cannot linger
So here it goes on my little finger.

Johnson collection/RTE

Life in Taylor's Lane, off Marrowbone Lane in the 1950s

Before Christy Smith got round to white-washing it off, every child in the street had it off by heart.

We never knew who owned the tenements, because an agent always collected the rents, so complaints and requests for repairs had to be made to the agent who either never bothered to inform the owner or else the owner paid no attention to them. Occasionally, when things really got out of hand, our local handyman, Christy Smith, would clear the stuffed drains and lavatories, but there was never any daily cleansing done. Every year or so, Christy would go round with a bucket of red raddle and slosh great dollops of it all over the walls in the halls and stairways with a whitening brush. The red raddle was the divil for coming off onto clothes, and was a dead giveaway for the courtin' couples.

The *Daily Nation* investigations in 1898 did nothing except publicise and highlight the appalling living conditions in the city and fifteen years were to pass before they again became the subject of much debate. A dreadful tragedy occurred in Church Street on the evening of 13 September 1913, when two houses collapsed killing seven people and injuring many more.

A Committee of Inquiry was set up by the government to study the housing situation in Dublin and when it made its report, the committee criticised both the landlords and the Corporation for their indifference to the dreadful conditions in which the working people had to live. It pointed out that in many cases the landlords and the Corporation were one and the same people and the names of members of the Corporation who owned slum houses in the city were exposed.

Another housing inquiry, this time in the *Irish Press* of 1936, led to the setting up of a Citizens' Housing Council, a voluntary body, which made a report, again to the Corporation. In the same year, the City Medical Officer, Dr Russell, made a submission to the City Council to enable it to adopt a resolution declaring Marrowbone Lane a clearance area and recommended the demolition of houses in it and the nearby Robert Street, Dickson's Row, Dickson's Lane and Price's Row. The same recommendation was made about houses on the Coombe, in Meath Street, Francis Street, Earl Street, Cork Street, Thomas Street and Poole Street, but the tenements in Pimlico, which were surrounded by all of these, weren't mentioned. The upshot of this last investigation did lead to the demolition of some of the houses in Marrowbone Lane and in 1938, 112 new Corporation flats were built on the site, but many of the people who had been born and reared in the demolished houses were scattered to the four winds. A lot of my mother's relations and friends were rehoused elsewhere and those few who were lucky enough to get accommodation in the new flats complained about having to live next-door to strangers.

Hard Times

When my granny left school she continued to work as a monitor for a time in both Meath Street School and Brown Street. The school in Meath Street was attached to St Catherine's RC Church and had been built during the curacy of the Rev Patrick (Canon) Duignan somewhere between 1816 and 1829 to replace a school for poor children in the parish which had been conducted in rooms which were unsuitable and dilapidated. To supplement her small wages she sang at local parties and functions and wrote personal letters for neighbours who had relatives abroad in England and America and she wrote business letters for tradespeople who were illiterate.

She was about twenty years of age when all the big changes began to take place in Pimlico, from the Coombe end up to the beginning of Tripoli. This was when the Corporation had cleared much of the area and gave permission to the Artisans' Dwellings Company to build houses and cottages. Six years before this the court-house, which had been lying empty, was taken over by James Darby, the clog- and shoemaker, who opened it up as a factory. He and his brother also owned clog and shoe factories in Cornmarket. In 1884 James Darby died and some time after that the court-house opened up as the Thomas Court Theatre, where granny trod the boards as a singer.

In the year 1887, when granny was twenty-six years old, she got married to Edward Kennedy from No 8 Braithwaite Street, who was a tobacco twister in Taylor's factory in the corner of Engine Alley and Francis Street. The following year my mother, Margaret, was born in the Coombe Hospital, the first member of the family not to be born at home. Granny got her own room in No 35 Pimlico beside her mother, Bridget, and her Uncle Michael. The house was now mainly occupied by Connollys, Coynes and Kennedys, all related.

Granny's next child was a boy, named Edward after his father, as was the customary thing to do with first sons, but when he was three years of age, he and my mother got typhoid fever, from which she recovered but he died. My mother's father lost his job in Taylor's and had to emigrate to Scotland to find work, where he died while my mother was still quite young.

On 20 June 1892, five days after my mother's fourth birthday, her grandad James Coyne also died at the age of forty-seven years. He had been forced to give up his job as a bellman long since, because of chest and heart trouble. The hard strenuous work of humping heavy sacks of coal on and off the cart, up and down flights of stairs, and sitting on the cart in all weathers finished him.

When it was time for my mother to go to school, she didn't go to School Street like all the others in the clan. Instead, granny took her to Brown Street where she was working at the time. Before going to school every morning my mother delivered milk just as her own mother and grandmother had done in their schooldays. In other ways my mother got more attention in the family because she was the youngest. As they were all very fond of music, someone bought her a mouth organ and in no time at all she learned to play it very well. A neighbour named Tommy McDonnell taught her how to play the melodeon and so the family then bought her a concertina. Before long she was playing with all the other local musicians at the open-air ceilis which were held up the Square in Pimlico in the fine summer evenings and at hooleys and weddings.

In 1897 when my mother was nine years old, James and Lillie Connolly and their children came to live in No 54 Pimlico. This was a large tenement house down on the Banks, at the corner of the Green Yard. There were six other families living in the house, the Farrells, Brennans, O'Donnells, Mulhollands, Cummins and Peels. Mr Farrell was in the United Labourers Union and knew Connolly well, and on the day Roddy was born, February 11 1901, Mary Brennan helped Lillie through the birth. Roddy's arrival brought the number of people living in the house up to thirty.

Uncle Paddy, my granduncle, was now thirty years of age and was working as a labourer in the brickworks in Dolphin's Barn, where it was not an unusual sight to see women working as hard as the men pushing large wheelbarrows full of bricks from the kilns. During periods of unemployment he had gone to work in Liverpool and Scotland doing roadwork, digging trenches for sewerpipes, in the course of which he had become very interested in trade unionism. At home in Dublin, James Connolly was his idol.

Swift's Alley looking towards Francis Street with Taylor's Tobacco Factory on right

Dickson's Lane off Marrowbone Lane looking towards Robert Street

When my mother left school she went to work in Jacob's Biscuit Factory where she was employed as a packer. Her Aunt Maggie, her senior by ten years, was a weaver in Mitchell's in Brabazon Row and Uncle Christy was employed in Judd's skin yard. Uncle Paddy was still in the brickworks, granny was out doing cleaning and scrubbing and the great-granny was working at housework. Between the lot they didn't earn one decent week's wage — it was just enough to keep the wolf from the door, but only for a while. The great-granny's health was beginning to fail, and she was finding it very difficult to move about. Eventually she was confined to bed with chronic rheumatism, and she died on 11 August 1911 aged sixty-six.

Uncle Paddy mourned her passing greatly. He had spent more time in her company than any of her other children and with her departure went his last link with the Irish language. Fifteen days after her death a strike took place in Jacob's and as the workers were marching through the city for more pay, they were baton-charged by the police in Parliament Street and many of them were injured. The strike was over in a week, and on the morning that the workers clocked back into the factory it was surrounded by a force of police. My mother said the workers resented being treated like criminals entering a prison.

Strike fever seemed to have hit the city in 1911 and it was notable for the number of boys who went out. Many of the strikes arose because the employers refused to recognise the trade unions, which were attracting increasing numbers of workers. One very interesting strike involved the schoolboys of St Catherine's School in Meath Street, who were striking for cheaper books and shorter hours. This strike started in East Wall National School and spread to Meath Street and John's Lane in the middle of September 1911. An attempt was also made to involve the boys of Francis Street Christian Brothers, but this failed. In Meath Street only thirty-three out of a total of 160 attended classes, while the rest picketed outside carrying banners on which were inscribed the words 'Strike Boys' and 'Cheaper Books and Shorter Hours'. The strike was shortlived and ended with the arrest of a fourteen-year-old boy from the East Wall School.

This strike focused attention on the inability of the childrens' parents to pay for schoolbooks and on the punishment which the children were subjected to for not being able to pay. Another strike at the same time by the bakers left the city without bread and the poor people were forced to buy potatoes which became scarce and went up in price. Even the cows were affected by the bread strike, because Mary Russell, who had a dairy yard in Marrowbone Lane, was prosecuted by the Corporation for selling milk which had been deprived of its fat content by twenty-five per cent. Mary said that her cows were always fed on cotton cake, but owing to the bread strike she had to feed them potatoes instead. She was let off with a warning.

After the 1913 lock-out, my mother wasn't taken back into Jacob's and there began a long period of unemployment and a very lean time for the family, because Uncle Paddy was out of work as well. To make matters worse, the terrible conditions under which he had worked all his life were having the same physical effects on him as they had had on his father. He could no longer wield picks and shovels or push heavy wheelbarrows and he could only move about with the aid of a stick. He put in for the Relief and took to sitting at the open window uttering derisive commentary on the state of the nation to the passers-by down below.

Over the years the Protestant population in Pimlico was steadily declining, which was possibly due to some intermarrying with Catholics, some leaving the street and others simply lapsing from attendance at church. The religions mixed freely, socially and at work, although in some jobs, notably Guinness's and Jacob's, the Protestants tended to have the cushier jobs. It was still the same in Jacob's when I worked there in 1948, but resentment about this was never directed at the workers who were in no way to blame. A Protestant family lived in one of the Artisans' Dwellings right opposite us and one of the boys in the family was making affectionate overtures to my mother. However, it came to nothing, not for religious reasons but for political reasons. Their allegiance to the British crown was more than our family could stomach, but they were much more tolerant of our views because the young man proposed marriage.

In the 1901 census, the total number of people living in Pimlico is recorded as 518, out of which 459 are down as Catholics and fifty-two as Protestants, the remaining seven being unaccounted for. The total number of farmsteads and outbuildings were twenty-four, which included eight piggeries, eight fowl-houses and two stables, the rest being sheds, workshops and stores. In the 1911 census, the number of people living in the street had risen to 607, out of which only twenty-eight are Protestant and if we include Mr Carter, an engine driver who lived with his family, six in all, in No 4 Pimlico Cottages (the Square), this would bring the number up to thirty-two Protestants. The number of farmsteads had also gone down to ten and the number of piggeries to two.

During the 1914–18 war, some of the young men in Pimlico joined the British army and went off to fight, some out of loyalty, others because they were unemployed or wanted a bit of adventure. Those who returned were either shell-shocked, disabled from wounds or suffering from the effects of gas. All of them got what everyone else described as 'good pensions' and those who could work got good permanent jobs as well. During the Easter Week Rising in 1916, Watkin's Brewery in Ardee Street just at the top of Pimlico and the distillery in Marrowbone Lane were both occupied by the Irish Volunteers, under the command of Eamonn Ceannt. A number of women were with the garrison, and after the surrender they were marched up to Kilmainham Jail, where they were imprisoned for a week. They were released on 8 May, the day on which Eamonn Ceannt was shot.

The family was now reduced in numbers to granny, her brothers, Paddy and Christy, and my mother. Granny's sister Maggie had got married to Johnny Balfe who worked as a dairyman for Kevin Barry's uncle, and the Connolly cousins had moved off to a bigger room in the area.

One day in 1918 my mother dropped a bombshell which shattered the family and caused a great deal of worry and heartache. She said that she was leaving home and was going to live with Jack Moorhouse, a married man with a family, whose marriage had broken up. The Moorhouses were an old established family who had lived in the Liberties for generations. Their names first appear on the register of St Catherine's Church, Thomas Street, in the year 1680. They lived mostly on the Coombe, having come over from England with the woollen workers, plying their trade until the import restrictions imposed by the English parliament reduced them to penury. In the 1800s some of them married into Catholic families on the Coombe, and gradually the records of marriages and christenings shifted to Francis Street and Meath Street chapels. One Protestant member of the family was the headmaster of the Mill Street Ragged School between 1865 and 1870. This house had at one time been owned by the Earl of Meath, after which it was rented by the Christian Brothers who later moved to Francis Street.

My mother and Jack Moorhouse went to live in 'foreign parts' on the far side of the Liffey in No 20 Mountjoy Street, where my eldest brother Sean was born. Within a year they were back in the Liberties and took up residence in Maria Lynch's lodging-house in Newmarket, where Paddy was born. Jack Moorhouse, my father, was a carpenter by trade and had worked in both Arigho's and Bull's, two church furnishing firms. Early in his working life, while working for Bull's, he had made the wooden frames for the Stations of the Cross for St Catherine's Church in Meath Street. These were removed in 1980 by the parish priest, Father Fogarty, who very kindly let me have one before they were sold for scrap.

The room in Newmarket was very small, and as my father was unemployed, Maria Lynch offered them a larger room in Whitefriar Street, in her other lodging house, where my mother worked at cleaning the house and collecting the rents. This helped to reduce the cost of their room from ten shillings and sixpence a week to one and six. Three more children, Jimmy, Stephen and myself were born here in No 26 Whitefriar Street, my advent into the world being in January 1931. All during the recession of the late 1920s, when unemployment was very high and getting worse, we were almost destitute. As well as having to provide for us my father also provided for his legal family, which doubled the burden and reduced him to a state of desperation, so that even when he was working we had very little. Money had to be got somehow and, pocketing his pride, he took to singing in the street.

This happened when Sean was seven and Paddy was five years old. They were both attending Clarendon Street School, and every day my father would wait for them outside the school and off they'd go to earn some money. During the week their route took them around the Baggot Street area and on Saturdays they toured Stoneybatter or the Ranelagh area. Street singers were ten a penny so they weren't such an unusual sight as they proceeded slowly along the channel, the boys on either side of my father, singing patriotic ballads on Ireland's rights and wrongs and the sentimental drawing-room songs which were popular at the time.

It was humiliating beyond description for my father to have to do this, because he took great pride in the fact that he was a highly skilled tradesman, whose father had also been a skilled worker in Spences Engineering firm in Cork Street where all kinds of machinery for brewers, millers, distillers and railways were made. He was further humiliated one day when a woman came over to him in Baggot Street and asked him all kinds of questions, particularly about the boys. She turned out to be from the Society for the Prevention of Cruelty to Children, and this Christian lady went straight down to the police and put in a complaint against my father. The police arrived and took them all down to the station, where after more questioning he was let go without being charged.

Engine Alley looking
towards Meath Street and
below, Storey's Villas,
Marrowbone Lane

Shortly after I was born my father's legal wife died, and on 21 August 1931 my mother and father got married in the Church of St Michael and John, in Lower Exchange Street. Granny was a godsend during the years of unemployment and without her my mother said that we would have ended up in homes. She got odd bits of jobs, cleaning and scrubbing, which enabled her to provide us with occasional half-pounds of butter and quarters of tea, and she got two loaves of brøad for us every day in Clarendon Street Convent for nothing.

In 1932 the city was alive with excitement in preparation for the Eucharistic Congress and there was a great demand for wooden window-boxes to brighten up buildings and houses. This gave my father a bit of work and much-needed money. His health was rapidly deteriorating, and a few weeks after the Congress celebrations he died, on 7 July 1932 in Whitefriar Street, eleven months after marrying my mother. Her cup of sorrow was not yet filled, because three months later, on 24 November, my brother Jimmy died in the Adelaide Hospital, as a result of a fall from the wall of Whitefriar Street School. He was just eight years of age and my mother sank down into the depths of despair from which she never fully recovered. Granny took over and brought us all back to Pimlico where the family, neighbours and all my mother's old friends rallied round and helped in every way possible.

Granny got us a tiny back room on the ground floor in No 33 Pimlico for one and six a week. We had no furniture of any description and there were no boards on the floor of the room, just earth. Paddy went up to live in No 35 with our two granduncles, which helped to relieve the congestion in our little room, while at this time granny was staying with a friend, Teresa Owens, in a house in Usher's Island.

Sean was thirteen years old and had left school. He got himself a job as a messenger boy in the Snack Sandwich Service in Wicklow Street, delivering sandwiches for five shillings a week. There was no such thing as the widows' and orphans' pension, so my mother had to apply for the Home Relief. The relieving officer, Mr Lawless, came round from the dispensary in Earl Street to investigate our circumstances and to satisfy himself that we were deserving cases. He interrogated my mother as if she had committed a crime by becoming a widow and having all these children that the state would now have to provide for. He gave her a card and told her to call to the dispensary the following Wednesday and collect two and six and warned her that if she gave any false information she would be liable to a hefty fine or imprisonment.

In desperation my mother applied to the St Vincent de Paul Society for help. Two men came this time to investigate and gave her two and six, but seeing that her situation was so bad that she was likely to be a constant drain on their resources, they began pressurising her into putting us into Artane Industrial School for boys and Goldenbridge Convent for girls. There we would be assured of a good Christian upbringing as well as food and shelter. My mother couldn't believe her ears so she politely told them not to bother coming again, that she would manage.

Unlike my mother, granny had no hang-ups about looking for charity when things were bad. When she was finished her few hours work in the Victory Café in Castle Market she'd slip round to Clarendon Street Convent for the two free loaves, then belt back to Pimlico, pick up a jug and trot down to the Little Flower Penny Dinners in Meath Street and bring back a jug of steaming stew. She was now seventy-one years old and the rushing around was getting too much for her, so she decided to move back to Pimlico.

As we had no bed and no floorboards, we were forced to doss down among the wildlife on the earth with sacks and coats to protect us from the damp. Everything that crawled, with or without legs, shared the floor with us. Eventually the rent collector, Maggie Vaughan, got the local handyman, Christy Smith, to put down floorboards. Then Mrs Fowler, who lived up over us, sold us a big iron bed with brass knobs and bars for a pound, which we paid for by the week. Uncle Paddy gave us a dresser and he made us a form of deal wood which seated three and

Nanny Devesey, the shopkeeper, gave us a butter box which was made into a fireside seat. This became my mother's most treasured possession, because it also held all her reading material.

Mrs Douglas, who lived across the hall in the room opposite us, was a home dressmaker and she measured up the window and made us curtains out of scraps of material. The dog-box was beginning to look a bit more comfortable.

Uncle Christy was working in Judd's hide and skin yard in Hendrick Street, and he asked my mother to do their housekeeping. His boss, Mr Judd, was an exceptionally kind man, and when Christy told him of our circumstances he increased his wages. Sean now had a job in the Wicklow Hotel and when my brother Paddy was just fourteen years old he got Sean's job in the Snack Sandwich Service, working as Sean had done from nine o'clock in the morning until eight o'clock at night, with a half-day on Wednesday, for five shillings a week.

Author's mother in 1947 aged 59 years. Photo taken by Jeromes of Henry Street

It was 'God help you' in those days when you got sick and needed medical attention, because our local dispensary doctor was a holy terror. Her name was Dr Tore and she was so unsympathetic and tyrannical in her dealings with the poor that Uncle Paddy christened her Dr Tory, 'a Tory by name and nature,' he would say. Everyone was so terrified of her that we would leave a sickness go until we were nearly at death's door before seeking medical attention. It was no wonder that we died like flies.

She hated coming to the people's houses on sick calls, so the dispensary would be packed with people suffering from illnesses of every description, all huddled up together on the bench in the waiting room and standing round the walls. It was a generally held opinion that if you had one disease going in, you had several coming out.

The dispensary, which was in South Earl Street, was a most depressing building on the inside, and anyone not feeling a hundred per cent became worse on beholding the decor. The upper walls of the waiting room were painted with a deep cream distemper and the dado was a middle brunswick green, with a line of dark brunswick green in between. Earl Street was very narrow, and even on the brightest of days the light was unable to penetrate the dispensary windows because the houses in Griffith Terrace and the large tenement house opposite blocked the sun's rays.

The floor inside was bare boards, and they gave off the smell of cheap disinfectant. Two wooden benches with no backs, one for the relieving officer's hatch and the other for the doctor's room, were at opposite walls. In the cold weather the walls felt like ice and were soaking with condensation. Between the relieving officer's hatch and the doctor's room was the apothecary's hatch.

The relieving officer sat in a room peering out at the people from behind the protective wire mesh on his hatch, which also had a little wooden door. He gave the impression that he was giving away his own money, and that all the poor recipients were there under false pretences. As each person handed in their Assistance Card he would scrutinise them with a cold, sharp look; then he consulted the card to see what amount was due. 'Mary Kennedy, two and sixpence,' he would shout out for all to hear. This was to let everyone know what each person was getting so as to encourage informers in cases where people were getting the Relief who weren't entitled to it.

Suspicion and fear were instilled into the people to such an extent that those on the Relief were afraid to talk to each other as they slid on their backsides along the bench towards the hatch. To make sure that he wasn't being diddled, the relieving officer paid regular visits to the people's homes. As soon as they'd open the door he'd walk in about the place, casting his eyes around. 'Any change in your circumstances since I was here last?' he'd ask sharply. If he saw anything of any value, he'd tell the people to sell it and he'd force them to do so by refusing assistance.

On the bench outside the doctor's room the scene was quite different. The sick in mind and body, old and young, sympathised with and consoled each other. Ailments and cures were debated as coughs, colds and diseases were passed on. Nearly everybody clasped an empty medicine bottle with a cork stopper, and anyone who hadn't got one suffered agonies in case they'd be refused the medicine, which often happened. It all depended on the mood of Dr Tore or the apothecary.

Each patient had to knock on the doctor's door before entering and close the door behind them on leaving. Dr Tore, who was in her middle years, sat behind a desk, and as each person knocked she let out a bawl, 'Come in — come on — put out your tongue — have you got a bottle?' No matter what their ailment everyone got the same cure-all. During the 'Emergency' there were terrible outbreaks of scabies, itch and impetigo, particularly among schoolchildren, and my brother Stephen and I fell foul of the itch. When we went in to Dr Tore and my mother told her we had a rash, she let out an almighty bawl, 'Get away from the

Coombe showing St Brigid's School and Convent on left, also J. Parkes, 1932

table, stand over there. Hold out your hands.' She told my mother to pull up our sleeves and unbutton our clothes and she then gave a long-distance diagnosis. During my entire childhood, I only had her visit me once and that was for measles, which in those days was a killer for poor children.

When I was three and a half years old my mother thought it was high time that I got from under her feet. As well as that she was anxious to get me away from the unhealthy surroundings of the tenement. Being cooped up all day in a small room measuring seven feet by nine or running wild out on the street wasn't her idea of proper child-rearing.

Stephen was already going to St Brigid's National School on the Coombe, where he had been transferred from Clarendon Street, both schools being under the Sisters of the Holy Faith. It was granny's decision to send us to the Holy Faith nuns because the children got a hot meal every day, so when the school holidays had ended after the summer of 1934 I was frogmarched off down to the Coombe screaming and bawling my head off. I will never forget that long walk up from the big school gate to where the yard opens up round the corner on the left.

Stephen was in Miss Devaney's class at the top of the lane and I was taken across the yard to Sr Mary Rose. My mother gave her all particulars, that I was toilet-trained, was four and a half years old, very obedient, and dying to go to school, not one word of which was true. Then she was gone with the promise that she would call for me in a short while.

Deserted and terrified, I looked up at Sr Rose who was dressed in the strangest garb I had ever seen. Her face was completely surrounded with what looked like a white cloth, with only her eyes, nose and mouth visible. She seemed to have no ears. She had thick horn-rimmed glasses and her head and shoulders were covered in a big black veil. Her chest was covered with a stiff white board in the centre of which hung a big cross with a brass figure, naked. Her long black frock reached to the ground and round her wrist she wore an enormous rosary and a wide, long, black leather strap. Tears filled my eyes and one of my mother's lies was exposed as a pool of water appeared at my feet.

Sr Rose's face remained stern, her eyes showed no sign of friendliness or understanding and I feared the worst. She put out her hand, bent slightly and took mine, and led me over to a table with a doll's house and said in a very quiet voice, 'You may play with that until you are tired, then you may sit down in that seat beside that girl. Her name is Frances.'

Left alone I tried to compose myself, puzzled at the turn of events. I had never seen a doll's house before and I was fascinated. After a few minutes I took the courage to look around the room. The walls were covered with lovely pictures of animals, funny people and writing, shelves with lots of books, a blackboard and easel, and lots of wooden desks, most of them with two children. Sr Rose sat at a table, nodding at mothers as they brought in victims like myself. Some were cutting up rough as they were flung inside by their mothers, but they seemed to know where to sit. I soon I learned that they had started a few days before me and that I was the newest recruit.

Sr Rose reached out, and with the palm of her hand she pressed a bell several times until the hubbub in the room stopped. She motioned to me to sit down beside Frances and then she took out a big, long book and commenced calling out names in Irish. She was very surprised when I answered 'annso' to my name and later on was more surprised when she discovered that I could count up to ten in Irish. The reason was quite simple — my brothers had already wised me up about the roll-call and Uncle Paddy who taught me how to count could only do so in Irish.

When the bell rang again we all stood up and trooped out in twos to the big yard. We were made to hold our partner's hand and be absolutely quiet. We marched up the yard, up to two long steps the width of the yard, turned left under a big stone stairs with iron bars and queued up outside a room from which came a most delicious smell of food. As we moved along inside we each picked up a tin plate and spoon and a woman filled our plates with stew from a huge saucepan with a big ladle. I couldn't believe my good luck and I nearly ate the plate, and when I saw some of the children going up for more, I went up too. We were allowed to play in the yard after this and Frances showed me the lavatories and the drinking water which shot up in the air, and told me the names of some of the children.

When my mother came up to collect me, Sr Rose gave her a good report. Thus ended the first day of the eleven years I was to spend at St Brigid's School. I was reluctant to go and I was more reluctant to leave. My mother came with me that first day and she never came near the school again until the day I left. She didn't like nuns and didn't wish to be involved with them in any way.

Granny certainly had her head screwed on when she insisted that we go to St Brigid's, because every Christmas we were given a food docket for Pigeon's grocery and provision shop on the Coombe, right opposite the Coombe Ragged School. Pigeon's meat factory was up in Coombe Street, close to Keeffes the knackers. There was one occasion I remember when they were summoned for unhygienic conditions in the factory. The dockets were for varying amounts depending on the family circumstances, and they were limited to those in real need. I can't remember when we stopped getting them but it was probably at the beginning of the second World War.

One day, my friend Frances, who lived in Coombe Street, wasn't in school and next day when she came in she was all togged out in a new brown frock and a fine pair of shoes. She wasn't too comfortable in the frock which was made of a flannelette material and was making her itchy, and the shoes were cutting the feet off her because she usually came to school in her bare feet. I was amazed at the brand new clothes, because her family was even poorer than ours and we had to buy all our clothes second-hand in the Iveagh Market or over in Cole's Lane.

'Where did you get the new clothes?' I asked.

'Them's the Police Clothes,' she replied. 'We get them every year, don't you?'

'No, never heard of them, where do you get them?'

'From the police. Your mother has to go down to the station and she gets a form and then the policeman comes to see her and then you have to go down to Pearse Street to get fitted. That's where I was yesterday. Me and Biddawan, my little sister, got them. Hers is blue. The only thing is now you can't pawn them because there's a stamp on the frock and look at the soles of the shoes.' She turned up each foot and indented into the sole were the letters CP. 'That means that they can't be pawned. They won't take them in the pawn, me mother tried, and Mr Murray in Ardee Street wouldn't take them. Anyway, you get arrested if the pawn takes them and you are found out and you never get any more clothes either.'

I thought that I'd never get home to tell my mother the glad tidings. New clothes for nothing weren't to be sneezed at. It was really the shoes that took my fancy because I had never had a new pair of shoes. My poor feet were tortured in second-hand boots and shoes and I always looked a holy open exhibition. My mother looked at me with her head sideways and her eyebrows raised. 'You may let it out of your head that I'll have anything to do with the polis. Be heavens, I'd rather go barefoot first. As long as I can afford the one and six or two bob for a good pair of brogues in the Iveagh I'll never go near the polis. Anyway, them oul' clothes are like a pauper's outfit and everyone knows that you're a down-and-out.'

I decided to take my case to granny because she didn't look at things in the same way as my mother, but to my surprise and disappointment she adopted the same attitude. Not only that, but she knew the whole history of the Police Clothes which went back as far as 1896. It seems that Lady Meath had been one of its founders and that it was a scheme which was already in operation in England before starting here. Granny remembered several cases where some poor unfortunate women were convicted and fined ten shillings or got fourteen days imprisonment for pawning the clothes. Apparently, the clothes were only lent and not given to the poor, so they weren't entitled to dispose of them.

Murphy's pawnshop, Ardee Street minus its golden balls

Nearly everyone in our street went to the pawn, and not just the people in the tenements. It was known as 'the poor man's bank' in some circles or 'me uncle's' in others. On Monday mornings, Mr Murray's in Ardee Street would be packed with women staggering under the weight of men's suits, shoes, watches, clocks, blankets, sewing machines, children's clothes, ornaments and gramophones — in fact anything they could carry. Even people who had good jobs in Guinness's and Jacob's or any other kind of steady employment frequented the pawn office. Some of them didn't like being seen going into it and they'd ask my mother to do the necessary. She didn't mind doing this because it wasn't like begging, so she would bring down whatever valuables they wanted to pledge in a bolster case and they'd give her sixpence for doing it. She had two good friends who were the 'lavins' of the betting office. Both their husbands were ex-British army pensioners with jobs who knew nothing of their wives' betting habits or their dealings with the pawn-broker. They were comfortably off compared with other families around, but their addiction to betting and gambling and fortune-telling reduced them to the pawn office every Monday. On Saturdays the pawn would be packed again with women and children redeeming their husbands' suits for Sunday. Some of them never got the money together to redeem the articles and they'd end up selling the pawn ticket or just letting the articles go. It was a pantomime in there sometimes, because the pawn-brokers and their assistants would engage in banter with the women as they haggled over the money. But there were sad times also when articles got lost by being given away to the wrong people, so it was essential to keep an eye to business when redeeming pawned goods.

Every Friday night the Vincent's men came around to dole out the few ha'pence or the clothes dockets. We would be posted on duty in the street and as soon as we saw them coming we'd dash up to whatever hall we knew they were visiting and we'd roar up the stairs the warning cry, 'the Vincent's men are coming.' This was the signal that anything in the line of food, clothes or ornaments was to be hidden. As we were children we thought this was very funny, but in actual fact it was a terrible indictment of the charitable societies' view of us. We were at all times expected to project the image of total destitution. Any effort on our part to improve our impoverished condition by making the home more comfortable when possible was penalised by the withholding of the handout. Simply to be poor wasn't enough, we had to act poor, and that was one of the reasons why my mother wouldn't look for charity.

In 1936 the widows' pension was introduced and my mother became eligible to receive the princely sum of seven shillings and sixpence for herself, three and sixpence for Stephen and one and six for me a week. It was no bonanza, but it was a step in the right direction. The pension was means-tested and every so often an inspector would call to question my mother on any other income. One of the questions which always amused us was 'Have you any land?' which seemed superfluous and we living in a dog-box.

My one abiding fear during my childhood was that my mother would die and that we would all be sent away to industrial schools or orphanages. This had happened to numerous children whose mothers had died, even if their fathers were still alive. When Mrs Murphy down on the Banks died all her children were sent to Artane. Mr Murphy worked in Keeffes the knackers and he was unable to take care of the children. They were sent to the industrial school, but he had to pay for their keep. Other children were sent to industrial schools and reformatories for the most trivial reasons, such as non-attendance at school and petty thieving. These cases were heard in Morgan Place, and Judge Little, who presided over them, knew only four words — Artane, Glencree, Daingean and Letterfrack. During the summer holidays, when some of the children came home for a few weeks, they would have to continue wearing their school uniform because they had nothing else. Playing around the streets with us they would feel very self-conscious because the clothes were like the badge of infamy. When Mary Stanbridge's son, who lived in the house beside ours, was sent to Artane, his mother couldn't afford the bus fare to visit him and it was only with the help of the neighbours that she could do so now and again. For the poor children who were sent to the wilds of Wicklow or Galway visiting was out of the question and the effect this had on the children and their parents was heartbreaking to see.

The charitable institutions and organisations certainly helped to provide sustenance and relief to the poor and the destitute, a few of them without asking too many questions, but the fact that these institutions existed at all was a reflection of the poverty of ideas, concern and motivation among politicans to tackle the problems of unemployment, bad housing, sanitation and health.

Among the people themselves there existed the most genuine support and neighbourly assistance. We lived in each other's ears. We depended upon each other for the 'lend of the loan' of a cup of sugar, an egg, a few spoons of tea, or a drop of milk. We loaned each other clothes to go to Mass or to go looking for a job. This idea of sharing was instilled into us from childhood and anything we got, such as sweets, biscuits, fruit or money, we were made share out. To say that a person was good-natured or 'a dacent poor skin' was the highest praise, no matter what other faults they might have, and the most charitable person of all was the one who would 'give you the spit out of his or her mouth'.

Rere of No. 54 Pimlico where James Connolly lived, showing Johnny Malone and Margaret Doran on their wedding day

Granny and Uncle Paddy

Granny was a very funny little woman in both appearance and manner. She was more serious and reserved than her two brothers, Paddy and Christy, or her sister Maggie, who was full of fun. Granny had little to say except when annoyed, when she had plenty. Being the eldest in her own family, with her mother only seventeen years her senior, she was used to taking charge and she reigned in authority over us all, and was totally dedicated to the task. In her latter days she spent a lot of time muttering softly to herself or humming bits of tunes and every night she would sit praying quietly, slipping her large rosary beads through her fingers. She prayed especially for two people, my eldest brother Sean, who was her favourite, and herself. The Hail Mary was intoned until she came to 'Holy Mary, Mother of God', when she'd raise up the voice in supplication, just to make sure that her plea was heard up above: 'Pray for me a poor sinner, now and at the hour of my death, and don't forget to look after poor Sean on that oul' messenger boy's bike, Ah-men.'

Nearly all the old women in Pimlico wore black shawls, and the remainder wore black coats and hats, except the granny, who wore a black cloak and bonnet. She wore several skirts all at the same time, which reached down to her ankles. Her feet and legs were encased in button boots up to her knees, with thick black stockings, under which she wore grey woollen coms. It took her ages to button the boots with a long buttonhook. Watching her undress was like watching someone peeling an onion — layer after layer of black woollen skirts, red flannel petticoats and ganseys, until eventually she came to the shift and the combinations, which were secured around her waist with an enormous cord. She had a very strange way of walking, which was no wonder with all that lot to carry, tripping along with short steps and giving the impression that she was about to fall flat on her face any minute.

She used to lose her rag with us whenever she found us lying and lolling in bed in the mornings instead of getting up for school. She would go on and on about when she was a youngster and had to be up at four and five o'clock in the mornings, hail, rain or snow, winter and summer, and had a day's work done before she went to school. She had to foot it up to Fairbrother's field or Mooney's field to milk cows and deliver milk, and after that rush home to help her mother wash, dress and feed the younger children before bit, bite or sup passed her lips. 'Be heavens, childer nowadays don't know how lucky they are having to go to school until they are fourteen years of age,' she would moan. 'In my day, what you had to do was go to work. You only went to school if and when you could, and no one gave a rollickin' damn if you never went.'

She was very proud of her bit of education and at school she had been regarded as a 'splendid scholar'. Like her mother, Bridget, she had attended School Street School, which had a very good reputation as an excellent teaching establishment. Children from all over the city came to it and it was open to all denominations. When granny was a pupil there her parents paid half a crown a quarter, but there was no hard and fast rule about the amount, as some paid more and others less. It depended on the family circumstances.

School Street School began from very humble origins when the vicar of St Catherine's Church in Thomas Street, the Rev J. Powell, opened a Sunday school for the children of the area on Sunday 23 January 1786. Only ten children turned up on the first Sunday and on the following Sunday twenty-four arrived. By the month of May, the numbers had increased to 276 with six masters and three mistresses. The applicants became so numerous that the school committee recommended that not more than six of each sex should be admitted on each Sunday as new scholars. Eventually it became so overcrowded in St Catherine's that it was necessary to divide the children, so the girls remained there while the boys attended at the Court-house of St Thomas.

It was obvious that there was a great demand for a better type of schooling and so it was decided to build a new schoolhouse in the area. The contributions for this came from all sources, mainly Protestant and Quaker, but Catholics also contributed and a piece of land was acquired at the corner of Crilly's Yard and Gilbert's Alley on which the new schoolhouse was built. It was known as the Dublin Free Dayschool.

In 1798, a year of great importance in the annals of Irish history, when the national rising of the common people for full civil and religious liberty was taking place, the new school opened its doors, and hundreds of children of all religious denominations entered its portals. In the early 1880s a new system known as the Lancaster system of education was introduced from England, where it was already in operation in a free school in Southwark, under the direction of Joseph Lancaster, a member of the Society of Friends (Quakers).

School Street School, formerly Dublin Free Day School. Opened 1798

In the 1850s one of the most famous pupils of the school was John Devoy, whose family lived in Newmarket, off the Coombe. He was a very bright scholar and he became a monitor in the senior class for which he was paid ten shillings a month. Granny also became a monitor in 1870, which seemed to be a cheap form of semi-skilled teacher. There was a wide range of subjects taught in the school and, apart from the three Rs, the children also learned music, drawing, book-keeping, geometry and algebra. Opportunities were afforded for the separate religious instruction of the pupils.

When Uncle Paddy, my granduncle, was four years old he was taken to the school with granny and apparently went willingly enough. However, he was a very disruptive child in the classroom and refused to speak English. He was tolerated for a while in the hope that he would improve but he continued to sing and talk as the fancy took him, until finally he was expelled. Given that this was a very enlightened school, his carry-on must have been out of the way altogether. As there was no compulsion on his parents to send him to any other school he stayed at home and remained illiterate, which he was to regret all his life. At home he was in the company of his granny Honora and his mother, both of whom spoke Irish to him, and until his mother died in 1911 they conversed together in their native language.

His lack of schooling didn't hamper his love of learning and in fact those who didn't know he was illiterate thought he was a very learned man. Every day when his two sisters and brother came home from school he would get them to read to him and he committed to memory all the poems and stories in their readers. This practice was continued all through his life and when he grew up it included getting them to read novels and newspapers. I remember he would sit at the open window holding a newspaper, pretending to passers-by that he was enjoying a good read, but sometimes the paper would be upside down. We used get a great kick out of going over to him and turning the paper the right way up. 'Your paper is upside down, Uncle Paddy,' we'd say. 'Oh, you're quite right,' he'd reply, without batting an eyelid.

Uncle Christy's schoolbooks were kept until Uncle Paddy died in 1943, when my mother threw them out because, she said, they were only cluttering up the place. Now and again, Uncle Paddy would get a yearning for the old stories and poems and he'd say to Christy, 'Kit, would you ever get out the oul' schoolbooks and read us a bit of Tennyson or Goldsmith.' Christy would get out one of his Blackie's Irish Readers and station himself over at the mantelpiece, on which stood the big brass oil lamp. With the light peeping over his shoulder, he would go through poems and epics, while Paddy's lips repeated every line. One of his favourites began

Oh, a rare old plant is the ivy green
That creepeth o'er ruins old.

Uncle Paddy had a nice, pleasant, roundy face, a thick moustache and a baldy head which he kept covered with a hard hat. Until he died at the age of seventy-nine he had all his teeth. The smell of tobacco hung around him like a veil and I thought it was lovely. During the weekdays he wore a muffler around his neck, but on Sundays he wore a stiff white collar with a brass stud in the back and another in the front which used drive him mad trying to fasten. He walked with great difficulty due to sciatica and arthritis, and he could only get about with the aid of a walking stick.

When I was young I was often left in his tender care, and some of my pleasantest memories are of the times spent listening to him singing his funny songs and nonsense rhymes as he tried to amuse me, dandling me up and down on his 'good' knee. He would try to get me to say 'Anna, Maria, Satia, Matilda, coal-box, ankle, heels, McGrath, soot', which had neither sense or meaning. Another was, 'The juice of an apple, the oil of a plum, hen's cac-caw, and monkey's dung'. To the tune of Paddy McGinty's Goat, he would sing

> Paddy McGinty, he bought a penny doll,
> He washed it and cleaned it and then he let it fall.
> He sent for the doctor, the doctor wouldn't come,
> Because he had a pimple on his bum, bum, bum.
>
> Oh, there was a little man and he had a little gun,
> And up the chimney he did run,
> With his belly full of fat and an oul' tall hat
> And a pancake tied to his bum, bum, bum.

This one may have been intended to dispel the fear of ghosts by showing how easily they could be disposed of:

> Johnny get your gun there's a ghost in the garden,
> Lying on his back with his belly to the wall.
> Johnny got his gun and his gun was loaded,
> Stuck it up the ghost and the ghost exploded.

One of my favourite rhymes was

> Johnny Mason broke the basin,
> What'll I do, said Johnny Drew,
> Rub it with oil, said Johnny Doyle,
> How much will it cost, said Johnny Ross,
> Half a crown, said Johnny Brown,
> Put him in jail, said Johnny Neal,
> Do you dar', said Johnny Maher,
> Aye, in a minute, said Johnny Sinnott.

Uncle Paddy smoked a clay pipe with 'T. Cunningham, 127 Francis Street' stamped on the bowl. He had another clay pipe, but it was broken, with 'J. Daly, 17 Francis Street, Dublin' stamped on its bowl. His good pipe, which he smoked on special occasions was made of briar, and it had a lid with tiny holes. It seemed to me that his briar pipe gave him a bit of bother because he was forever scraping the inside of the bowl with a penknife and sticking pipe-cleaners up the stem. When he wasn't smoking tobacco he was paring it into thin slivers with the penknife or else chewing it in his mouth, but, smoking or chewing, he was forever spitting into the fire or out the window.

Liberty Creche, Ireland's first creche opened by Quakers

Maternity and Child Care

When I was a child, which was long before television brought sex to Ireland, our mothers acquired babies in a variety of ways. Some of us were found under heads of cabbage, others were bought for sixpence in Woolworths, while more were brought in the doctor's big, black leather bag. Whatever about the way we came I always knew when one more had arrived by the heavy, sickening smell of ether which would penetrate the entire tenement, lurking for days in every nook and cranny.

For some unaccountable reason mothers always took to their beds when the new babies arrived. I was ten years old before I knew why. The babies had a strange habit of coming in the middle of the night, causing great inconvenience and confusion all round. If there were already young children in the family they were dispersed among the neighbours, while all sorts of comings and goings took place. The prospective father would go to a nearby relative or spend the night pacing up and down the hall, depending on how experienced he was at becoming a father or anxious at the turn of events.

The connection between ether and babies was slowly dawning upon me when a tragic event took place which opened my eyes to reality. Mrs Crosby was a neighbour who lived in a small top-back room in our house. Her husband was a soldier in the Irish army and was stationed mostly in the Curragh, but he came home quite often at weekends. She was constantly pregnant, but some of her babies were premature and died, or her pregnancy might sometimes end in a miscarriage. My mother was always on call because she felt particularly sorry for Mrs Crosby who was suffering from TB and looked like a walking skeleton.

She had three children, all of whom were born upstairs in the back room. The two eldest, Chrisie and Mikey, were pals of ours although younger than us. The smell of ether seemed to cling to Mrs Crosby perpetually and her constant racking cough went on night and day. She died one night in childbirth, leaving now four young children. My mother broke down in sorrow and I learned the mystery of life. Chrisie and Mikey and the two smaller children were taken away and put into orphanages and not only did they lose their mother and home, but they lost each other, for they were sent to separate homes. Shortly after, the mother of a schoolfriend died in the Coombe Hospital and a terror of childbirth gripped me.

Home confinements were very common in those days, and at the rate at which the children were born a dozen maternity hospitals wouldn't have sufficed. As it was, proper pre-natal care and attention for the mothers and babies just wasn't available and far too many children were born suffering from deformities and other ailments, which in many cases could have been prevented. Under the Medical Charities Act, provision had been made for the grant of free medical and midwifery attendance to necessitous women, and each year thousands of cases were attended at confinements in their homes by the medical staffs of the Dublin maternity hospitals. The number of home births kept rising each year until 1937, when figures began to show that more Dublin mothers were beginning to attend pre-natal clinics, which were provided under the Dublin County Borough Scheme, and to avail of the maternity hospitals for their confinements.

Giving birth was indeed very dangerous in those days. One of the most dreaded diseases of childbirth was puerperal infection, which was the dominant cause of maternal mortality, and from 1932 to 1936 inclusive there was a decided upward trend in the numbers of mothers dying from this disease. But from 1937 onwards there was a continuing decline in the numbers of deaths which coincided with the increase in attendance at clinics and the decrease in home confinements.

Improvements were also due to the widespread use of the sulphonamide group of drugs and the extra care which was taken with midwives who had been in contact with the disease. Their throats and noses were swabbed, and if haemolytic streptoccoci were found they were suspended from attending other confinements while they might be liable to transmit the infection.

For the babies born during the 1930s, as I was, surviving the trauma of birth was only the beginning of a hard battle for life. No sooner were we launched into the world than we were struggling against the most terrible odds. Our main enemies were diarrhoea, diphtheria, scarlet fever, measles and influenza. My mother's generation had had to contend also with typhus and typhoid fever, and both my mother and her younger brother, Ned, contracted typhoid fever, from which he died.

In 1936 there was an enormous increase in infant mortality, representing a rate of 74.15 per 1000 births, the highest since 1926. The Medical Superintendent Officer of Health, Dr Russell, said that it was due to diarrhoea and gastroenteritis, and he blamed cow's milk, carelessly handled during the course of transit from the cow to the infants. He advocated breastfeeding as the simplest and most effective preventive measure. Two years later, in 1938, the Medical Officer's Report regretted that very little progress had been made in the reduction in infant mortality and he now added strikes and economic stress, bad housing and the failure to breastfeed as large factors in keeping the rate high.

No reason was given in the report as to why the mothers weren't breastfeeding their babies, but a survey among Dublin mothers showed that sixty per cent of them were unable to. Maybe if the Medical Officer had come around Pimlico, Marrowbone Lane, Earl Street and the Coombe he might have got a better insight into the problem. Only twice did I see a mother breastfeed her baby when I was growing up. Our mothers used crescent-shaped bottles with rubber teats or soothers at both ends, and they had so many children to look after that they just hadn't the time to sit down and nurse a baby and anyway they would have needed half a dozen breasts to keep up with the demand. It was a very common sight to see a baby propped up in a pram or cot sucking a bottle of milky tea, well laced with plenty of sugar, or to see a little toddler ramming the bottle down the baby's throat, while at the same time sucking its own bottle.

After a baby's birth, the Jubilee Nurse would come around daily to attend to the mother and child. She was a very familiar figure around our street in those days with her navy blue gaberdine, little navy hat, black shoes and stockings and the black leather bag which held all her medical equipment. Sometimes she arrived on a bike and we would all rush over to her to ask if we could mind it for her and as soon as she disappeared into the house we would have 'goes' on it up and down Pimlico. The Jubilee Nurses' full title was The Queen Victoria Jubilee Nurses because they were incorporated by royal charter in 1889 and endowed by Queen Victoria with £70,000. When the Jubilee Nurses came to Ireland in 1890, St Patrick's Home for Nurses affiliated to it, but unlike their counterparts in Britain, Irish nurses had to pay £50 to enter the large Dublin hospitals and the superintendent of the Irish nurses was always appointed from England and was usually a Scottish woman. These nurses were so kind that they were known around our way as 'angels of mercy'. There was absolutely nothing they wouldn't do, and so they always got a great welcome from the kids as well as the parents.

Because so many babies died soon after birth we were in the habit of getting the christening done as soon as possible so that the little soul wouldn't have to wander forever in Limbo, which was a very lonely place to be in. Limbo must have got overcrowded, because I never hear of any babies going there now. The babies were all dolled up in flowing white gowns and shawls and were carried to the church by the godmother. They wore little white bonnets, and anyone who couldn't afford the robes was always given the loan of them by the neighbours. After the christening the godmother carried the baby in her arms around to all the relatives, neighbours and friends, and the lucky infant had its little palm well greased with pieces of silver. This handsel was to bless it with good luck and prosperity for the future. Some godmothers found this awful thirsty work and they'd keep nipping in and out of the snugs for bottles of stout or something stronger, squandering the infant's handsel and ending up hardly able to hold the child. In some cases the godmother would do some of her rounds before the christening, and as a result many a child ended up with a strange name, as in the case of my granny.

As soon as the mother got to her feet after the birth, her first duty was to go to the chapel to be churched. This was a thanksgiving service after safe birth and although in theory it was voluntary, all the mothers, when I was young, felt that it was compulsory, and in a sense it was, because social pressure forced women to go. The generally held view of churching was that women had to be cleansed after giving birth, implying that in some way it was dirty. Many women resented this, and found it a complete contradiction to other Church precepts, which elevated marriage and procreation to a state of grace. Prayerbooks in my youth referred to it as a 'pious and praiseworthy custom' and in my mother's time the ceremony required that the woman kneel at the entrance of the church holding a lighted candle. The priest would then touch her with the end of his stole and introduce her into the church with prayers and holy water. Over the years this changed and it was no longer necessary for the mother to stand at the church door, but one thing didn't change and that was the attitude of the Church to unmarried mothers, because this blessing wasn't given to them. My own mother would have been excluded for this reason, but in any case she didn't like the idea.

Old Coombe Hospital, the Coombe, founded in 1826 by Margaret Boyle

Women had a hard time of it always, because the whole burden of bringing up the children in overcrowded conditions and without enough money to see them through each week, fell on their shoulders and although you won't find it in any statistics, many women had to go out to work to supplement the family income. In fact, in a lot of cases where women were widowed, deserted or their husbands were unemployed or unable to work, the woman's earnings were often the only income, which occasionally was supplemented by the Relief or St Vincent's. There were always women who traditionally worked such as dealers, tuggers and paper-sellers, and in such households, their children worked too.

This had been the situation in the Liberties for generations, so much so, that the Society of Friends (Quakers), in the year 1794 provided the mothers in the area with what is now the oldest creche in Ireland. The name over the door in Meath Street reads, 'Sick Poor Institute and Liberty Creche'. As well as providing day nursery facilities 'for the children of respectable women who are dependent on their own exertions for support', the Friends helped to provide for the sick poor of the Liberties whom they visited in their own homes. Without their help many of the older generations in the district, such as my great-great-grandmother and her descendants down to my granny, would have suffered in times of sickness much more, because the local dispensary in Earl Street wasn't opened until 1866. As always, though, unmarried mothers were discriminated against because they received no help and they couldn't leave their children in the creche.

I visited the creche many a time when I was about ten years old, although I was never inside the front door. One of my pals was a paper-seller and she lived in Belview Buildings. Mary was the eldest of eight children and her parents and three other children were also paper-sellers. Hail, rain or snow, they had to set off every morning and evening to collect and deliver the *Herald* and *Mail*, the *Irish Press, Independent* and *Times*, and the only ones with shoes on their feet were the parents and Mary.

The four youngest children had to be taken to the creche every day and Mary's mother asked me to do the necessary. All the children were what we called double-jointed, which meant that from the knees down their legs were bent outwards. This was a condition properly known as rickets and was caused by a lack of vitamin D and malnutrition. It was very prevalent in my youth, and I remember my mother used to buy large jars of codliver oil and malt in Daddy Nagle's, which I thought was delicious but other children thought disgusting. The second youngest child in Mary's family was totally crippled and was only able to push himself along on his backside so he had to be wheeled or carried. The family had no pram, only a wooden boxcar with two shafts for pushing, and in the centre there were two old pram wheels with no tyres. The wheels were kept on by sticking used matchsticks in the axle holes, and every time the matchsticks broke the wheels flew off. I used be crucified trying to keep it on an even keel as I sped from Belview to Meath Street with the four kids piled into the boxcar, and every so often I would have to stop and search the channel for another match.

The door of the creche had iron bars on the lower half which came out in a rounded shape, intended, no doubt, to prevent children from standing up on the door panels and scraping off the paint. The irons are now gone, but the holes in the door are still there as testimony to their past existence. In response to my ring a young girl wearing a white starched apron and cap would open the door only just wide enough to allow in the tiny body of a child. I would leave my charges in early in the morning, hungry and unwashed, but when I called for them in the evening they would emerge spotless, well-fed and rested. My recollections were that this only cost sixpence a day for one child with reductions for additional children. It was a blessing for the mothers who were lucky enough to find places for their children, but as in all such cases the demand was great and the majority of mothers had to fall back on relatives and neighbours to childmind.

Older children in families were often kept away from school to look after babies and it was the cause of many a child being sent off to an industrial school for being constantly absent. The courts showed no mercy or understanding, and young children were torn away from their homes to spend years under the harsh discipline of Christian Brothers and nuns. A letter in the *Evening Mail* of Monday 4 July 1938, under the heading 'The Hidden Ireland of the Poor', cited the case of a young child who had been sent away to an industrial school. His mother had kept him at home because another child in the family was dying. The child died on 4 February and the boy was sent to an industrial school on 4 March. We lived in constant fear of being sent away to schools and I knew many who spent their childhood in Artane, Goldenbridge, Letterfrack, Daingean, Glencree and other houses of correction.

Difficult as it was in those times for many families, unmarried mothers and their babies were even more disadvantaged, and so they suffered most of all. They were subjected to the utmost humiliation by society, and many of them were totally rejected by their families. Those who were evicted from their homes gave birth to their babies in institutions which were run by various religious orders. Friends of mine whose parents stood by them had their babies in St Kevin's Hospital, which was still referred to as the Union. In the religious institutions there was little or no sympathy shown to the mothers, who had to earn their keep by working themselves almost to death in the sweltering heat of laundries for long hours and under atrocious conditions. They had to work right up to the birth of the baby and immediately afterwards. They spent long and many an hour down on their knees scrubbing and polishing floors and performing all kinds of tasks which were totally unsuitable to their condition and dangerous to the babies.

The infant mortality figures speak for themselves and they tell a shameful story. In 1933, when I was only a baby myself, the death-rate among children born to unmarried mothers was three and a half times greater than among those born to married women. Local Government Reports for 1935 and 1937 show that the mortality rate for the babies of unmarried mothers was 260 per 1000 births, which was greatly in excess of the rate for babies born to married mothers, which was sixty-two per 1000.

In an attempt to improve the situation, the Public Assistance Authorities, through the National Maternity and Child Welfare Grant, gave financial aid to homes for unmarried mothers. In these homes, arrangements were made for the mothers to care for their babies for a certain length of time, after which suitable foster homes were found for the children by approved agencies. I knew some 'nurse children', as they were called, who were very happy with their foster-mothers, but they lived in dread of being taken away and sent somewhere else, while there were others where the 'suitable home' left a lot to be desired. Compared with nowadays, it was very easy to foster a child, and any of them I knew were fostered by middle-aged women living on their own in tenement rooms.

My own mother was of course strictly speaking an unmarried mother for most of her 'married' life, but she and my father were accepted as a couple by the community. Far from being rejected, my mother had the full support of her mother and family, and my father was well liked by my mother's family. However, there was always a fear at the back of my mother's mind that we children might be taken away from her, because by being unmarried she might be considered an unfit mother. This was one of the reasons she avoided charities that had associations with the Church.

Local Characters

Sartini was a big, powerful man. His physical proportions and social standing were gargantuan. He wore a large hound's-tooth tweed cap, a sports jacket with large loud check squares, plus-fours and multicoloured diamond-patterned knee socks.

He rode an enormous upstairs model cycle, the saddle of which was off a motorbike. It had three wheels, two in front and one behind, and fitted across the handlebars between the two front wheels was an ice cream container. On the handlebars he had a big black horn which he put to good use to announce his arrival in the street.

He never ever got off the trike to serve the ice-cream. He rose up from the saddle, stood on the pedals, leaned over the handlebars, lifted the lid partly off and scooped out the ice-cream for the cornets. He had a gadget for marking the blocks for the wafers and a container with raspberry colouring which he squirted quite liberally on the ice-cream for sheer good value. As soon as we saw him swinging into Pimlico on his ice-trike we would start singing:

I know Sartinio, he sells ice-creamio
All around Pimlico and left me on my ownio.

He didn't like being jeered and, forgetting that we were his potential customers, he'd give chase on the trike, mounting the footpaths trying to jam us into the wall.

At one time Sartini lived in Taylor's Lane and half-owned a second-hand bookshop around the corner in Marrowbone Lane. The other half was owned by his friend Spud Murphy. Most of the books they sold were True Detective, True Romance, westerns and comic-cuts. They were also reputed to sell 'dirty books' and banned books, but in those days even the English women's weeklys, such as *The Oracle, The Miracle, Peg's Papers* and the *Red Letter* came under suspicion and were occasionally confiscated lest they contaminate our innocent minds. The shop was raided a number of times, and once, on the foot of a warrant, the police swooped in force, threw all the books out onto the cobble-stones in Marrowbone Lane and set fire to the whole lot.

However, Sartini had many irons in the fire and the loss of a few books didn't put him in the Union. Along with the bookshop he had a rag-store, which stood on the site where Marrowbone Lane Flats were later built. His other pursuits were money-lending, blackmarketeering in Sunday night cinema tickets and betting.

Sartini was one of two boxmen who ran the toss-school up in the Greenhills, beyond Griffith Bridge. Like a ringmaster in a circus he stormed about the centre of the toss-school circle wielding a short-handled dray driver's whip. The lash of the whip was about three feet long, and Sartini would use this mercilessly to enlarge the circle so as to enable the other boxman to get the bets down for the tosser, who would then throw up the two 'makes' off the 'feck'.

The 'feck' was a little bit of a stick about the width of a ha'penny and the length of the fingers. The 'makes' had to be thrown over the head or else the throw was an illegal try. Bets were unlimited on the inner ring and as much as the tosser put down had to be covered before the boxman looking after the tosser allowed the 'makes' to be tossed. He would then call out in a very loud voice the result of the toss so that those on the outer ring could hear. Two ones, head and a harp, meant that the tosser had to toss again. Two heads meant that the tosser had won so everyone placed bets again. Two harps meant that the tosser had lost his bet. The toss-school was very popular on Sunday mornings and many a hard-earned week's wages took wing.

One day a bellman with a dray full of coal lost all his readys in the school and then bet his load of coal against the tosser heading the 'makes' again — but he lost. The unfortunate man went completely out of his mind and tried to commit suicide. He flung himself into the canal to drown his sorrows, but several members of the toss-school hauled him out and then proceeded to beat the living daylights out of him. Their only concern was to avoid any publicity which would reveal the school's existence to the police.

The kind of wheeling and dealing which went on in the underworld inevitably led to occasional outbursts of violence. For some reason, the Animal Gang from Ash Street came up to make an attack on Marrowbone Lane and School Street. Leading the gang was a woman. Sartini mobilised his forces when wind of the word was conveyed to him by runner. He was ably supported by Tommo Finn, a fine big lump of a man from Neill's Court in Marrowbone Lane, who laid about him in swashbuckler style with a 1014 sword which Johnboy Lannon had unearthed up in the tiphead. It had helped Brian Boru to defeat the Danes and it brought luck to Tommo Finn. Knives, iron bars, knuckle-dusters, chains, lead piping and razors were all used. The battle took place at the corner of Marrowbone Lane and Pimlico. The residents of Pimlico kept well out of sight, although we had a grandstand view from behind our closed windows. The Animal Gang were beaten and retreated sucking their blood. Sad to relate there was a dreadful sequel to this feud when, shortly after, an innocent man named Mickser Gill from Maryland, being mistaken by a member of the gang for someone else, was stabbed and died outside Russell's dairy in Marrowbone Lane.

Owen Doherty, known far and wide as Doco, was our local vet, not that he ever did an hour's training in any college. From near and far owners of all kinds of animals came to him for advice and help, his love and knowledge of animals was so legendary.

He had an ass called Lucy which he bought from Doyle's in Marrowbone Lane for half a crown and he carried it, cradled in his arms, to his house down on the Banks. He also had a roan pony called Silver and a terrier called Pops. Lucy was used for collecting the pig-swill and Silver for going to the coal yards and for delivering the coal. Pops also joined in these expeditions, trotting behind between the two back wheels. Her job was to prevent the lads from scutting on the back of the dray, because Doco never used a whip. They didn't have to anyway, because he let them drive the drays and many of them got their experience of traffic and later jobs as carters through Doco's apprenticeship.

We called him Doco-No-Toes because of the peculiar way he had of walking on the balls of his feet. This peculiarity was supposed to be due to the fact that he was a boxer and had won many amateur medals. However, we really believed that he had no toes. His brother Sikie was a welter-weight champion and they both ran the Belview Club in Thomas Court Bawn, which later moved up to the Connolly Pipers' Club beside Thomas Street Library. They were responsible for training many good boxers from round about and footballers too. Among them was Bobby Lawlor, the bantam-weight, and Jimmy Tracey, an exceptionally good welter-weight.

Doco was very highly thought of by the locals generally and he was every mother's darling because he kept the lads off the streets and therefore out of trouble, and he was also very generous when weighing out the coal and blocks, throwing in the extra shovelful of slack when the scales went down.

One very strange recreation which he indulged in was the rat race which he organised now and again in Thomas Court. (This term eventually came into the language to describe fierce, unscrupulous competition.) All the dog-owners taking part would assemble at the bottom of Thomas Court and South Earl Street. The rats were brought in cages and each dog-owner laid bets on his dog catching a rat. The rats had two escape routes, a shore on either side of Thomas Court. Doco would stand about four feet in front of the dogs who were held by their owners by the collars, and at a signal he would pull up the cage door and rat and dogs sped into action. Good dogs were sold for high prices and were much sought after by men who were employed as rat-catchers by local firms.

One figure of fun and fear in our youth was a policeman from Newmarket Station whom we nicknamed Swally-The-Pig. He was of enormous proportions with a belly the size of a Guinness barrel and a face like a full moon in a fog. He was Public Enemy No 1. In spite of these disabilities he was very fleet of foot considering that he also wore a heavy uniform and a pair of very heavy brogues. His big fat head was stuck up in the hole of a tall helmet and in wet and wintry weather his frame was enclosed in a large cape. On his belt, just at his right hip, he carried a black leather case with a truncheon which had a life of its own when in his hand.

The boys always played football in the street and we all played handball up against the blank walls of the Square. The football was usually a pig's bladder blown up or a wad of newspapers tied with twine. Sometimes we knew when he was on the beat and we'd organise a look-out to keep nix but when the look-out fell down on the job, Swally-The-Pig would have a field day.

Every time we were caught he took our names and addresses and before long we were issued with summonses to appear in court. The fine was two and six, which in those days was an awful lot of money to us. He even summonsed the kids who were only looking on, and no amount of pleading innocence made any difference. His attitude was that if you weren't guilty today, you would surely be guilty tomorrow.

Belvue Football Team 1928

Gangs of corner-boys regularly stood holding up the walls of Guinness's buildings, and as Swally-The-Pig passed by throwing each leg out in front of him, his thumbs stuck under the buttons of his breast pockets and the strap on his helmet cutting into the flesh on his double chin, they would start whistling 'Harvey Duff' to match the beat of his feet. This tune was anathema to the police ever since the time of the Land League when people were arrested for whistling it after them. It became very popular again when I was young because Laurel and Hardy used it in their films. The tune was also used as a warning to the lads playing pitch-and-toss round the Bawn so that they would have time to disperse before the 'bluebottles' arrived. Every Friday and Saturday morning the Gallopin' Dealer ran all the way from the Coombe to Ma McCann's house, beside the Swingin' Boats, carrying on her head a huge basket full of fish or Jaffa oranges, depending on the day. She was a fine, big woman and wore a long black full skirt over which she had a snow-white bib with large pockets. Around her shoulders was a large black shawl and her feet were bare, except in winter when she wore men's boots.

Woman's work. Dealers in the Liberties bearing their burdens with grace and dignity

Ma McCann's was a private tenement, housing two generations of McCanns and another family named Russell, who owned dairy yards and cattle in Marrowbone Lane. The Gallopin' Dealer would open the hall door and run down the hall out to the back yard. Here she would drop the basket and strip to the waist and proceed to wash herself under the cold tap. She carried her own lump of carbolic soap and a clean cloth to dry herself. After washing and dressing herself she would let down her hair and 'rack' it with a big comb. Her hair reached nearly to the ground and with a few flicks of the wrist she would twist it into a bun, which she held in place with the comb. Her toilet completed, she would swing the heavy basket back up onto her head, fix the shawl about her shoulders and gallop up the Long Entry until she got to St Catherine's where she'd settle herself outside the church. She never smiled, rarely spoke and never called out the price of her fish or oranges.

The older people knew her well and would nod good morning, but I never saw her in conversation with anyone. She was the only character we never jeered because there was such an air of sadness and mystery about her.

By contrast, Mary-All-Papers was a tiny little woman, who carried an old oilcloth market bag full of papers of every description and we gave her a dog's life. She wore several coats and an old battered hat from under which her hair stuck out in wild wisps. She slept rough in tenement houses but now and again she would go missing and we would all think that she was dead. She was very friendly and was full of good humour in spite of her destitute situation. She got tea and sandwiches from Mrs Dowling and got a few pence from the neighbours. She was a sad little figure as she wandered aimlessly around collecting papers and bags to keep herself warm on the landings at night and on dry winter's nights she would get her sleep on Guinness's hot-plate in Rainsford Street. During the daytime she would queue up with all the other poor down-and-outs at the 'Berril' in Meath Street, which was an eating house run by the Society of Friends, who had their Meeting House in Meath Place.

Every evening at about half past four, Johnny Tynan, our regular paper-seller, came running round our corner at the Bawn, into Pimlico and down towards the Banks, yelling at the top of his voice, 'Hairy-Hiock-Nuk-Noc-Na-Mayoc'. That was his way of saying HerillerMail or HerillonerMail (*Herald* or *Mail*), which was the usual paper-seller's cry. Johnny's barefooted children accompanied him on most evenings but sometimes Mrs Tynan would join the race which began outside the offices of the *Herald* and the *Evening Mail*.

Johnny was a squat little man who wore a long, tattered overcoat which reached right down to the ground. Winter or summer he wore this coat because it was part of his working gear. His children were quite young and, hail, rain or snow, they never wore shoes. Their clothes were in bits and whenever Johnny could land them a blow he would.

Johnny would wait outside the *Evening Mail* office with all the other paper-sellers while Mrs Tynan and the children waited at the *Herald* office. As soon as the papers came off the press, Johnny would scoop up his quota in the tail of his coat and tuck the lot under his oxter and start running. Mrs Tynan and the kids were expected to catch up with him at some stage and God help them if they didn't. Up Cork Hill, into Christchurch Place, Cornmarket and all the way up to St Catherine's in Thomas Street the whole family ran, but they didn't all run in the same way. The children and Mrs Tynan sold the papers so they would dash here and there, crossing the road when necessary and stopping to collect payment. Johnny was the front runner and as he ran he doled out the papers to the others and yelled his paper-cry and when he wasn't doing this he was cursing and hitting them for not keeping up with him.

Paper-sellers only came around Pimlico in the evenings, the morning papers being sold in the shops. On Sundays Johnny Tynan never came around, we had Gollier instead. He was a tall, skinny man with a permanently runny nose and he was always spitting. He pushed his load of Sunday papers in a boxcar and although he sold the usual *Sunday Press* and *Independent* he did a roaring trade in *Reynold's News* and the *Sunday Empire*. The people loved the English papers because they had more murders and sex crimes than our own and they added a bit of spice to the Sabbath and gave it a bit more balance. Then a new paper-seller came on the scene named Christy. He was one of the nicest paper-sellers in Dublin and was very popular with the women because of his good humour and banter. Johnny Tynan eventually stopped coming around but Christy is still going strong.

As a child I was terrified of Bang-Bang. He lived quite near to us in Mill Street and later in Bridgefoot Street, so we saw a great deal of him. The minute I'd hear him approach I'd run for cover. All the girls were afraid of him but the boys loved to hear him coming, shouting Bang-Bang and shooting in all directions with his latchkey.

Our main objections to him were his demands for hugs and kisses, and if any of us were unlucky enough to get caught our hysterical screams brought our mothers to doors and windows, who when they saw it was Bang-Bang would join in the shoot-out. 'Lovely girl, lovely girl, givus a kiss, givus a kiss, bang-bang, you're dead, will you marry me, there's me wife, bang-bang.' In no time he would have the whole street in a state of siege. He always survived the shoot-out and in real western style he'd canter off down the street leaving the dead and wounded strewn everywhere, even hanging out through windows.

As he rode his steed into action he took little short skips, slapping his right side to urge himself along, while he held his imaginary reins in his left hand. He was very agile and could jump on and off moving buses without turning a hair, grabbing the bar at the back platform while aiming his key at the enemy.

He was innocent and harmless and was easily led into dangerous situations by the wild buckos who enjoyed his cowboy antics. One day, my brother Stephen, John and Powah Connor and Osso Doherty were playing a game of Dawn sitting under Mrs Connor's window down on the Banks when they heard Bang-Bang approaching. They started having a bit of fun and Osso took his key, which left him unarmed. Just then who should turn into the street from Gray Street only Jembo-No-Toes. It was an encounter fraught with danger, only poor Bang-Bang didn't know it.

Jembo-No-Toes lived only a short distance away in Garden Lane on the ground floor of a house facing Spitafields. He was supposed to be a shell-shocked ex-British army soldier and, like Doco, he walked on the balls of his feet. The door of his house was in two halves and Jembo would lean over the bottom half watching the world go by. He got on well enough with his neighbours, but he could be very abusive with strangers passing by and the children going to school in Francis Street were forever jeering him a for a bit of a skit. The neighbours would lodge complaints with the Brothers in the school who would beat the daylights out of them. Jembo was reputed to be the only man who rode a wooden horse in the first World War.

The boys immediately saw the dramatic possibilities created by Jembo's arrival on the scene. Osso was quick off the mark and he handed Bang-Bang back his key and pointed over to Jembo saying, 'He's the head crook. You be the chap and go down as far as Barretts and come up behind him. I'm the sheriff and I want him dead, right.'

Bang-Bang's face lit up with excitement and he did as he was instructed. He cantered up behind Jembo, who wasn't paying a blind bit of notice, and he rammed the key into Jembo's back. 'Stick em up. Bang-Bang,' he roared, and Jembo nearly had a seizure. He made a vicious swipe and let out an almighty roar at Bang-Bang who was absolutely delighted and made off into the air-raid shelter on the Banks. Jembo's blood was up and he gave chase threatening to break every bone in Bang-Bang's body. In one door and out the other, into the darkness of the shelter and out again, round and round they went, one shooting and the other cursing and swearing. Then somehow Jembo came across the end of an iron bed which had been dumped in the shelter, and he swung it at Bang-Bang. Luckily it didn't hit him, but it took an enormous lump of concrete off the entrance to the shelter. It was only then that Bang-Bang realised that Jembo was a real baddie and he made good his escape round Julia Hennessy's corner and up the Long Entry out into Earl Street. When Jembo got around the corner he had vanished and so he turned his attention to the boys who were now calling him names.

The 'King of Ballad Singers', John Wilson, a regular Pimlico visitor

Saturdays

Saturday was my favourite day of the week. It was all hustle and bustle and a wonderful air of excitement and gaiety hung over Pimlico. Very early in the morning the countrymen would come clattering over the cobble-stones, their great big hobnailed boots scraping the stones and sending sparks flying underfoot. Their trousers were tied at the knees with sugans (hay ropes), and they walked beside their horses, leading them down from the direction of Thomas Court, round by the Bawn and into Pimlico where they halted. They then fixed sacks which contained a well-earned feed of oats over the horses' heads, and started to sell their loads.

Their high wooden carts were painted a bright orange, with turf and cabbages piled high up into beautifully neat pyramids. As they had no means of weighing the turf it was sold by the sod, and several heads of cabbage could be bought for a penny. We were on great terms with the countrymen and they would let us mind their horses and give them carrots and buckets of water and they didn't mind in the least when we taunted them with:

> Your cart is racked and worn, friend, your ass is very old,
> It must be twenty summers since that animal was foaled.
> He was yoked in a trap when I was born, in September '83,
> And he cantered for the midwife, says the turfman from Ardee.

The area seemed to change character on Saturday and became more like a country market. Street dealers lined Thomas Street and Meath Street, and people seemed to come out from under the stones. Women strolled leisurely up and down the streets clutching marketing bags, and haggled with the dealers over prices. Cockey Roach at the corner of Meath Place and Julia Halligan at the corner of Crostick Alley did a roaring trade in vegetables and fruit, while Bridie Fay and Susie Doyle couldn't keep up with the sale of pigs' feet, ham-parin's, skirts and spare ribs. Great big barrels of brine stood outside their shops with pigs' heads, whole and half, and pigs' tails, and corned beef. All you had to do was to plunge your arm down into the brine and bring up your Sunday joint.

If, as they say, cleanliness is next to godliness, then we were a very religious people. The tenement houses were swept and scrubbed from top to bottom with buckets of carbolic soap and bottles of Jeyes' Fluid and Pine. The women in the Artisans' Dwellings scrubbed their granite window-sills and doorsteps, and washed the footpaths outside their doors. From mid-morning crowds went to confession, children were everywhere, the dealers sang out their wares, and banter and good-humour were all around. Windows were washed and brass door-knockers, keyholes, letter-boxes and handles were brasso'd till they glittered.

Saturday was a half-day for most working men and the pubs were packed to capacity from midday, all too many of them drinking the week's wages. It wasn't unusual for some wives and even children to have to waylay the men before all the money was gone on drink. My mother's Uncle Christy, who lived with us and worked in Judd's skin yard, would sing a snatch of a song whenever my mother told him to come straight home from work:

> When I get my week's wages to the shebeen I'll go,
> And it's there I'll sit drinking as long as porter will flow.

Taking advantage of the fair-day atmosphere and the captive audience, the ballad-singers did their rounds, strolling slowly along the channel, cap or hat in hand, collecting whatever could be afforded or selling ballad-sheets, which sold like hot cakes. Of all the ballad-singers who came around Pimlico, none could compare with John Wilson, who was a great favourite. His rendition of 'The Valley of Knockanure' was a pure joy to hear. All the windows in the tenements would go up, heads and half bodies would lean out, as he moved slowly down the street, his lovely rich voice giving real sincerity and meaning to the words. We would gather around him, moving at his pace, while the ha'pennies, thruppenny bits and sometimes even sixpences were tossed down from the windows. He never stopped to pick them up — it was our job to stop them rolling and put them into the leather pouch which he had fixed to his accordion with a hook.

Around his shoulders he wore an old leather cloak, which fastened under his chin and was open down the front. His accordion was strapped under this from his shoulders, and on his head he wore a battered slouched hat, cocked on the 'Kildare' side, which gave him a very rakish appearance. He also sold ballad-sheets, which were of different colours, by which means he was able to tell one song from another.

John Wilson was an itinerant ballad-singer and was well known throughout the length and breadth of Ireland. In a book entitled *Before and After Puck Fair* the author, Stower Johnson, pays him special tribute, and a large photograph of him can be seen at the annual Puck Fair Exhibition in Killorglin, which is owned by Pa Hourihan. In an article in *The Kerryman* in 1963, Bryan McMahon described him as 'the king of ballad-singers' and so he was.

After tea on Saturday we weren't allowed out. My mother would put on a good fire, fill the big black iron kettle to the brim with water and haul the galvanised bath out from under the bed. She then armed herself with a big bar of Sunlight soap, a fine-tooth comb and a towel or an old sheet.

The grooming would then begin. Our heads were thoroughly searched with the fine-tooth comb for nits and lice and then liberally douched with oil of sassafras. The smell was disgusting and the oil had a tingling effect on our heads. If the lice weren't stung to death they were certainly poisoned by the fumes. Those drawn out on the comb were given a sudden sharp end with the thumb-nail or given a cracking send-off in the fire. Inner cleanliness wasn't forgotten either, and skinny bottles of Californian syrup of figs, cups of senna tea, and chocolate worm cakes, covered with coloured balls, were forcibly administered.

This same ritual went on in all the families and was colloquially known as 'being battered'. The water for this operation had to be carried in buckets or jugs from the taps in the back yards of the tenements, so it was treated like gold-dust, especially if it had to be carried up several flights of stairs. As each child was 'battered' a drop of hot water was added, and the same water was used again for the next victim. This scrub-down was to make us look our best for Mass and the visits to grannies, aunts and other relations next day.

The Sunday best clothes were all laid out on chairs or left hanging on the ends of iron beds. Shoes were polished with Nugget or Cherry Blossom and in summer runners were washed and given a good coat of Snoween to spruce them up. They were then put out on the window-sill to dry with the supplication that Duckser Healy's pigeons wouldn't leave their message all over them.

As Saturday night wore on a carnival atmosphere was generated as the pubs filled up, the hooleys began and the 'ruggy-ups' erupted. Boxing matches were a regular feature after closing time and the fights broke out for the most trivial reasons and in the words of the song 'Finnegans Wake', it was woman to woman, and man to man. A lot of the ruggy-ups took place at our corner and so we had a grandstand view from our window.

Crowds would gather from all quarters, some trying to separate the combatants and only ending up getting a hiding from both. Others urged on their favourites. Coats, caps, shawls, shirts and ties would be discarded and thrown down on the ground with a vengeance, and the bodies would lock together, rolling about on the cobble-stones. Someone was always sure to go to Newmarket for the police and as soon as the lookouts saw them coming they would shout, 'Here's the Razzers,' and the crowd would scatter in all directions. When things really got out of hand the Black Maria would arrive and a squad of policemen wielding batons would drag everyone in sight down to the station.

However, for the majority of drinkers, the hooley was the usual way to bring Saturday night's carousing to a close. Someone was sure to find a reason for a social get-together in one of the tenement rooms. The drink was ordered from the publican and it was delivered to the house by a porter wearing a white apron. He carried a huge wickerwork basket with a leather strap which he wore over his shoulder like a school bag. The basket was laden with bottles of Guinness and spirits, and the unfortunate man had to deliver by shank's mare, all round the various streets and up and down several flights of stairs. The bottles in those days were made of glass and were money-back-on-return, so the porter would have to repeat the journey after a few days to collect the empties.

The singing, drinking and story-telling would go on into the small hours of the morning and those who had earlier had been knocking sparks off each other would roll home, arms entwined round each other's shoulders for support, proclaiming to all the world that they were

> Comrades, comrades, ever since we were boys,
> Sharing each other's sorrow, sharing each other's joys,
> Comrades when manhood was dawning,
> Faithful whate'er may betide,
> When danger threatened, my darling old comrade,
> Was there by my side.

Unfortunately, this Saturday night drinking had its tragic side too. More women and children were battered on Saturday nights than on any other night of the week by drunken husbands and fathers. While the police were quick to arrive on the scene to intervene and make arrests when members of the same sex were involved in a violent incident, husbands attacking their wives were ignored. The attitude of the law and the Church to battering made it more culturally acceptable, and so the victims had no support. A woman praising her husband might sum up with 'and he never raises his hand to me'.

Sundays

Church bells and cooking smells wafted together from early dawn on Sunday mornings. Beginning with the gentle tones of John's Lane at 6.30 a.m., each church in the Liberties would join in as the morning wore on until by midday the sounds would increase in volume to almost deafening proportions as the bell-ringers of St Patrick's and Christchurch took over the air-waves.

I loved the sound of the bells as they boomed, peeled, chimed and clanged almost non-stop, as one Mass or service was about to finish and another to begin. Coming from and going to church was a great social occasion with hundreds surging in and out, bidding each other the time of day and stopping to plan the day's activities.

Everyone was all dolled up in the Sunday best so that apart from performing religious duties the journey to and from church was like a fashion parade. I knew people who didn't go to Mass simply because they hadn't the clothes. Others went to very early Mass so as not to be seen by too many of the neighbours while others only went to Mass in order to show off the style.

My mother seldom went to mass when I was very young, and she finally gave up going altogether when one Sunday she was refused admission through the front door of Meath Street Chapel because she put only a penny in the collection box. Oul' Bennet the collector pulled her up and told her to go around the side door with her penny. She took back her penny and from then on she made her own arrangements with God. This custom of having a 'poor side' was detestable to those who couldn't put a thruppenny bit or a sixpence in the collection box and incidents between the poor people and the collector were quite usual.

Every Sunday at 10 a.m. there was a special children's Mass in Meath Street which every child in the parish was expected to attend. It's a good job they didn't because they would never have fitted in. The most popular Mass was the 12 o'clock in John's Lane with Dan McNulty the blind organist and the choir of the Augustinian seminarians. It was truly magnificent and more uplifting than any sermon.

It was customary for fathers to take their small children to Mass on Sundays and from there to trot around visiting grandparents, aunts and uncles who lived locally. Here the children would get the Sunday penny, the biscuit and lemonade and be made a great fuss of, while the mothers at home struggled over the hot stove or the damp turf fire trying to cook the Sunday dinner.

The smell of fry on a Sunday morning was delicious. For those who couldn't afford the rashers, sausages, onions and black and white pudding it was torture. Mostly the fry was only for the fathers or the older children who were working. My brother Sean always got a Sunday fry because he was the breadwinner, but the rest of us were allowed to dip a cut of bread in the gravy on his plate. It he was in a generous mood he would give us a bite of a sausage or a suck of the rasher rind but my mother, like all the other mothers, was quite strict about him being left alone while he ate his meals. Workers were privileged in our households — they needed more food to give them the strength to work.

After the breakfast the women set themselves the task of cooking the dinner which was a major operation. It was easier for the women in the Artisans' Dwellings because they had access to running water, sinks and gas cookers. In the tenements our mothers were crucified having to wash vegetables under the tap in the back yards and having to cook on open fires, while pots slipped and spilled and put the fires out. The houses reeked of pigs' feet, pigs' cheeks, bacon, cabbage and corned beef. Frying and boiling were the only methods of cooking. When the meat was nearly done, in went the cabbage on top. When it was dished up it was swimming in grease. A mug of this cabbage water with a cut of bread was doled out to any child unlucky enough to be around.

The leftover cabbage water was poured into a bucket with bits of stale bread and other scraps. This was kept for Hoppy Lawlor who had pig-yards in Marrowbone Lane. He went around every Sunday afternoon with his horse and cart, on which there were two large filthy drums, collecting slop for his pigs. The smell off the drums was a knockout. He gave us a penny a bucket of slop and these buckets were usually the same ones which were kept under the beds for sanitary purposes.

St. Catherine's Meath Street, showing station made by author's father

This disgusting swill was fed to the unfortunate pigs, who every so often succumbed to attacks of swine fever. A particularly bad outbreak occurred after the war and the Minister for Agriculture made an order prohibiting the use of such slops for the animals. In the next few years the piggeries in slum areas were closed down, much to the relief of the local inhabitants, whose olfactory organs were sorely tried with the malodorous stench from the pigsties.

After the Sunday lash-up we would call for our pals and head off for the Tivo in Francis Street, the Pheeno on the Quay or the Fountain in James's Street. If you were lucky enough to have someone in the house working you got regular pocket money. If not, the picture money was got by selling slop, bottles and jam-jars to Harry Sive in Crostick Alley or by selling cinders and bundles of sticks around the houses during the week.

The queue for the Tivo was an exercise in self-inflicted torture. We would all line up for the woodeners outside the lane in Francis Street. Pushing, shoving, skipping the queue and punch-ups were all par for the course, and it was usually the innocent who fell foul of the usher. The Pimlico gang always liked to see Tucker Upton in charge of the queue, because he lived next door to us in No 34 and we got favouritism. Tucker was a boxer by profession with the Phoenix Boxing Club, but his wife, who was reputed to be an Italian from the Coombe, was more than a match for him because she was a female Roman-Grecian wrestler.

The regular knocker-up and chucker-out in the Tivo was a big lanky oul' fella armed with a stick, which he put to good use on our bare legs. We hated and feared him but the weals which he rose on our limbs didn't stop our carry-on. As long as we got into the 'follinupper' we didn't care about the wounds he inflicted.

In those days the major-domo of the picture house staff always wore full regalia. This was a uniform with brass buttons down the jacket, gold braid on the cap, sleeves and trousers, epaulettes on the shoulders, which held snow-white gloves, and a cane carried in the hand. He strutted up and down the Tivo steps like a peacock in full display. His presence made us feel very important because his appearance added a touch of class to our neighbourhood.

The boys, who were football-crazy, would head for the Phoenix Park during the summer when the weather was fine and sunny and too warm for the pictures and we would sometimes put on our own concerts and entertain the neighbours. The concerts were held up in Mick Murphy's yard which was half way up the Long Entry on the right-hand side going from Pimlico to Earl Street. There was no end of talent knocking around, singers, musicians, Irish dancers, tap-dancers, all able and willing to show off what they could do.

The charge into the concerts was a ha'penny or a pin. The ha'penny entitled you to a cup of fizz or lemonade with the entertainment. The pin entitled you to the entertainment only. Nanny Devesey did a roaring trade in fizz-bags, lemonade and jelly-babies. Everyone had to bring their own cups and seating was for the grannys and grandas only.

A wooden door in the Long Entry opened into Murphy's yard, which contained four little white-washed cottages all of them with half-doors open at the top. Cocks and hens ran in wild confusion during the performances, while Mick's cat sat disdainfully on the half-door of his cottage. There was great rivalry between the pupils of our local Irish dancing teacher, Essie Connolly, and the pupils who went further afield to the Genocchi school and the Rory O'Connor school, each one trying to out-high-step the others.

Occasionally a ballad-singer would come around on Sunday afternoon, the most popular being Willie Gannon from Chancery Lane. He was well known in Dublin as a street singer of music-hall songs and was affectionately known as Charlie Chaplin because of his attire, which was a hard hat, baggy trousers, walking stick and old boots. Sometimes he wore a military jacket with gold braid epaulettes and gold braid stripes. In the summer he never wore anything on top except a tie around his neck. His repertoire was at times quite bawdy and he performed all sorts of dance routines, swinging the walking stick with great skill.

Willie loved audience participation. The audience leaned out of the tenement windows or stood at the hall doors singing along with Willie who accompanied himself on his melodeon. His favourite songs were 'At Trinity Church I met my Doom', 'Mick McGilligan's Daughter Mary Ann', 'Where Did You Get that Hat' and 'I Tucked her under me Oxter'.

Once we had performed our religious duty of going to Mass, Sunday was a day for relaxation and enjoyment, but for our Protestant neighbours it was a day of total prayer and devotion. The friends we ran around with during the week simply nodded at us as they passed us by at different times of the day on their way to Morning Service, Sunday School and Evensong. They went to St Catherine's in Thomas Street, Donore Avenue, Christchurch or St Patrick's and paid visits to each other's houses but between them and us there was an agreed separateness on the Sabbath.

How we spent our Sundays depended on the weather and the time of the year, but we were rarely bored. At times there seemed to be a constant stream of entertainment passing through with St James' Brass and Reed Band, swirling pipe bands, Boys' Brigade bands and religious processions.

On Sunday nights the courtin' couples went down town to the pictures if they were lucky enough to get tickets at blackmarket prices from Sartini. The tickets had to be booked in advance and there was quite a lucrative blackmarket trade. Going down town for a walk was a favourite pastime and hordes of factory girls with arms linked together would traipse around sporting their Sunday best, clicking fellas and window-shopping.

> And all around by George's Street, the loving pairs to view,
> Mary swanked it like a queen in a skirt of royal blue,
> Her hat was newly turned and her skirt was newly dyed,
> And you could not match her round the block down by the Liffey side.

For those more inclined to matters of the spirit, 8 o'clock Devotions in Meath Street or John's Lane or a ball of malt in the local, fortified them for the next week's hard slog.

> There's music in my heart all day,
> I hear it late and early,
> It comes from fields far, far away,
> The wind that shakes the barley.

The mouth organ was the most popular instrument in Pimlico when I was young, and Larry Adler was God. Nearly every child at one time or another was given a mouth organ to suck and blow as a substitute for the doh-doh. 'Between the roars of her and the bawls of him I'm nearly driven to distraction. Stick the bloody mouth organ in that child's mouth or I'll change its bloody tune with a box,' was an often-heard maternal lamentation. So, born out of the necessity to get some respite from ear-splitting screams, our mothers introduced us to the sweet sound of music.

My mother taught Sean to play when he was quite young, and by the time he had reached his teens he was brilliant. At night, to put me to sleep, he would sit by the fire and play my favourite tune and to the haunting strains of 'The Red River Valley', I was wafted into the land of nod. He graduated from a small sixpenny mouth organ to the larger, more elaborate ones with intricate key changes, which he bought with the money he got as tips in the Wicklow Hotel. Many show-business people frequented the hotel in those days, and one night, while a party was in progress, the barman pushed Sean out to entertain with his mouth organ. Jimmy Campbell from the Theatre Royal was very impressed with his playing and asked him to call around to the theatre for an audition. Sean was out of his mind with delight at first, but then he got cold feet and never turned up. A golden opportunity missed, perhaps, but then who knows?

Sean's passion for music was insatiable and one day he caused great excitement when he came staggering home under the heavy weight of a gramophone with a huge green horn. My mother didn't know whether to laugh or cry. 'In the name of God whatever possessed ye to buy that and we with not a bit a food in the place and that young one walking on the Cherry Blossom and she after gettin' murdered in school for not having the money for her school books or the black babies? Have ye no bloody savvy at all, child?' Secretly she was delighted because she couldn't wait for him to get it going. Everyone from the top of the house to the bottom was invited in to the first performance of Larry Adler, and from then on we had regular record concerts.

The gramophone was treated with the utmost reverence and respect. No one but Sean was allowed to play it and no one else but my mother was allowed even to touch it. When not in use it lived under the bed where it was safe from accidents, and at the same time it was away out of sight from the prying eyes of the relieving officer, should he pay an unexpected visit. Before each performance my mother would dust it down after placing it in the middle of the table and the needle was examined to make sure that it wasn't blunt. These womanly chores completed, Sean then took over the manly job of winding it up and announcing each record before putting it on the turntable. Many a time I stood at the hall door of No 33, feeling as proud as punch as the music filled the tenement and passers-by stopped to listen and enquire who owned the gramophone, while my belly was like a washing-board with wrinkles from the hunger. But then, man, or indeed woman, does not live by bread alone, as the women from Lawrence, Massachusetts, pointed out in 1912 as they marched through the streets singing 'Hearts starve as well as bodies; give us bread, but give us roses.'

Sean bought all his records from Cha Coleman's shop in Meath Street, at the corner of Crostick Alley. Mr Coleman and my mother were great friends and Sean was allowed to spend as much time as he liked in the shop listening to records, surrounded by bicycles and their accessories, books and magazines, which Cha also sold. Our taste in music was very catholic and the collection of records grew rapidly. Sean introduced us to military bands from all over the world, but his favourite was the No 1 Army Band under Colonel Fritz Brassi. We had Gracie Fields, the Flanagan brothers, Jimmy O'Dea, Grace Moore, John McCormack, music-hall, Strauss waltzes, concertos, sonatas and symphonies, as well as Irish jigs and reels. If it made a sound, we had it. Some of the neighbours bought records even though they hadn't gramophones and they'd bring them in to Sean to have them played, so everyone's tastes were catered for.

The street was full of talent, of which we were all very proud. Vera Dillon, who lived in No 31, beside the Long Entry, was the local Myra Hess. Her teacher, who lived down on the Banks, was Mrs Sharkey. On the wall outside her door she had a lovely brass plate which displayed her teaching qualifications and added a tone of respectability to the street. Vera's father was known as Kruger and had served in the first World War, where he had been badly affected by gas and because of the 'bronicals' he couldn't work. Her mother was a forewoman in Todd Burns factory in Mary Street and was locally called 'a right oul' targe'. During the afternoons, while Vera's mother was lambasting the unfortunate workers in Todds, Kruger would stand at the open hall door, coughing and gasping for air, while Vera practised her pianoforte. He was a very nice man and he would let us sit on the doorstep as long as we kept quiet. We were all as familiar with the works of Beethoven, Chopin and Mozart as we were with the works of Tom Moore. We all thought Vera was great and a famous future was predicted for her, but then she went and got married.

Our other female virtuoso was Kitser Ryan who lived down on the Banks in No. 56, in a small row of houses with little gardens in front. Kitser played the piano accordion and was a constant visitor to my mother who loved to have a go on it. Kitser was very thin and delicate and when she died in her teens from TB the whole street was saddened and my mother felt that she had lost another child.

Kitser's pals were the Hennessys from No 46 and, like Kruger, their father was an ex-British army pensioner whose loyalty to the British crown was notorious, but his daughters, Elly, Addie and Lily, were all champion Irish dancers. Their trophies filled the glass case in the parlour and their costumes were like suits of armour with medals. Their mother, Julia, was a cousin of Danny Cummins the Dublin comedian. His brother was a fireman up in Thomas Street Fire Brigade Station and like Danny was renowned for his wit. Our famous Irish dancing teacher, Essie Connolly, who now lives in Thomas Court, came originally from No 38 Pimlico, and the Traceys who later moved into that house had a son called Peter, who was a great all-round dance-band musician. Peter played the piano accordion, the clarinet and the drums in various dance bands and eventually ended up with his own dance band.

When Jemmy Gibney, the silk weaver, who lived over our room, moved out, Nan Murray and her daughter Bridie moved in. Every night they spent hours singing songs in harmony. Their repertoire was quite extensive, covering a whole range from music-hall, to ballads, drawing-room Victorian and opera. They accompanied themselves with the tapping foot, which used drive my mother insane because she couldn't concentrate on her reading. I loved hearing them sing and I learned many a song from them, although some of them made neither sense or meaning like

> Don't go about like a hen that wants to lay,
> You might be here tomorrow and you might be here today.
> Oh, that's what the jury cried, since we've all got troubles of our own,
> What a silly coon, he's looking at the moon,
> He's eatin' a cake and leaving the walk alone.

And another which went:

> Mad, mad, mad, completely off her dot,
> Drank a bottle of paraffin oil and thought it was whiskey hot.
> Mad, mad, mad, touched upon the brain,
> Mad, fairly mad. she'll never be right again.

Marrowbone Lane in the 1940s from the Widows Home to Mrs Furlong's Shop

The Bayno

Tip-toe to the Bayno,
Where the kids go,
For to get their bun and cocoa,
Tip-toe to the Bayno with me.

Going to the Bayno wasn't one of the regular activities of the children in Pimlico, but from time to time we would become very adventurous and we would sally forth from the security of our own environment to mingle with the hundreds of kids from all parts of Dublin, who would converge on the Bull Alley daily for their bun and cocoa.

We always had to ask permission to wander so far afield and almost invariably we'd be refused. There was always some excuse like 'It's too far away,' or 'It's too dangerous to be crossing Patrick Street,' or 'There's too many dirty oul' fellas in Patrick's Park,' or 'You'll get lost,' which I did one time in Nicholas Street when I was eight years old and was never let live down the shame. But we knew the real reason why our mothers didn't want us to leave the street. They wanted us to be on hand to run for endless messages or mind smaller children. The fact that I didn't have anyone younger in the family didn't make any difference because someone else's mother was sure to land me with the job of childminding, and besides, my own mother was always running out of snuff. My brothers used say that her nose was like one of the turf-banks up on the canal from sniffing her quarter-ounce of brown, which she kept in a Colman's mustard box deep in the pocket of her cross-over bib. The young fellas, on the other hand, were allowed free range and could roam as they pleased which made their lives much more adventurous than ours.

However, occasionally we would manage to escape the net of maternal role-casting and just for a change of scene and to broaden our horizons we'd head for the Bayno. It was an experience not to be missed, and for days afterwards we'd be falling around the place laughing ourselves sick at all the funny goin's-on and rituals, not to mention the skirmishes with some of the 'rossies'.

The Bayno was frequented mostly by the children who lived in and around the Bull Alley, and they had the same sense of ownership about it as we felt about our playground. There were times when we barely tolerated outsiders coming into our Swingin' Boats and woe betide them if we took it into our heads to bar them. It was like having a war between the Earl of Meath's gang and Lord Iveagh's gang with each one boasting that the facilities their lord had bestowed upon them was better than the other's.

The 'Bayno' was the colloquial name given to the Iveagh Play Centre, and was the Dubliners' inimitable way of saying beano, meaning a feast, the feast in this case being a bun and cocoa, which was doled out to the children daily. The Bayno in its early days wasn't situated in the fine, well-equipped buildings which I used to go to in the Bull Alley. Many years before my tiptoeing days began, the Play Centre was in 100 Francis Street, in a tenement house, just beside Mark's Alley. Here it began its life on 15 December 1909, with an attendance of fifty children. The word spread like wildfire that this was a great place to go to, and within a month the numbers had risen to 137 and then shot up to 918 children daily.

Now, royalty were forever dropping in on the people of the Liberties whenever they were here on visits, and the visit during July 1911 was no exception. On 8 July King George V and Queen Mary of England popped into the Coombe Hospital to see if we were still breeding, and sure it was no trouble at all to call around to the Play Centre in Francis Street. Everyone was wild with excitement as you can imagine, and the kids couldn't get over it. It was the highlight of the Play Centre's existence.

The Francis Street project was so successful that the first Earl of Iveagh, Edward Cecil Guinness, decided to build and equip a new Play Centre in the Bull Alley, which become part of his 1903 housing scheme, whereby the old, overcrowded Dutch Billys and other slum tenements were demolished and new, modern flats were built. They were called the Iveagh Trust Buildings and, just like the Artisans' Dwellings, they became much sought-after.

The opening of the new Play Centre took place on Tuesday 26 April 1915 and was a great affair. Among the notables was Lord Iveagh, Mrs Ernest Guinness and the Misses Guinness, Sir Matthew Nathan, under secretary for Ireland, and Lady Nathan, Mr Justice Ross and Mrs Ross of Bladensburg and the local parish priest Canon Scally.

The underlying idea was to provide education and amusement for the poor children of the slum tenements in a pleasant atmosphere, with opportunities to learn skills by using equipment which their poverty-stricken circumstances made it impossible they would ever own themselves.

On the day of the opening 600 little girls sang a number of 'appropriate songs in a manner which showed how carefully and successfully they had been taught by Mrs Fitzgerald, the Lady Superintendent and her assistants.' Sir John Ross of Bladensburg congratulated the children on having such a noble benefactor as Lord Iveagh. Canon Scally hoped that before long they would have a statue to Lord Iveagh in Patrick's Park, just as they had one to his brother in Stephen's Green and Lord Iveagh himself said that he hoped that they would enjoy the many and interesting things they were told and taught, which would enable them to grow up happy and useful women, and he hoped they would ever look back with pleasure on the happy days spent there. There were only girls there on the opening day, which was in keeping with the tradition of having separate days for the sexes, and the girls were given the honour on this auspicious occasion because it was considered that they would be better behaved.

It was in the 1940s that my pals and I used go to the Bayno, and on the way down we would always sing the Bayno song. It was very important to get down there in time or else you mightn't get in, but getting there too early wasn't the best plan either, because there was the danger of getting involved in gang warfare and some of the regulars would scrawb or reef you to bits if you looked crooked at them.

I think some of them were psychic, because by some unknown means they always knew when opening time was approaching and would start forming the queue. This was the flash-point when the queue-skipping, pushing, shoving, boxing matches and threats started.
'Wait till I get you outside the gate, ye common rossie ye. I'll lave ye suckin' yer blood.'
'You and what army?'
'Who do ye think yer lookin' at, cock eye?'
'Nothin' much when I'm lookin' at you, gunner eye.'
This kind of name-calling, hair-pulling, kicks in the shins and insults were all the norm and were indulged in by the usual few trouble-makers who could never keep their hands to themselves.

As soon as the door opened there'd be a great surge forward and a loud cheer. The heave would come from the back, and whether you wanted to or not you were forced into pushing the girl in front. It was like a stampede, and God help you if you tripped and fell. However, once inside the door, order would suddenly descend at the sight of the superintendent and her assistants, whom all of us called teachers.

While order was being restored and we were being formed into single file, the first girl would take up her position at the door into the main hall. Then as soon as the teacher opened the door, a piano at the far wall was pounded into action by another teacher. Then the first girl would lead us into the strains of Sousa's marching tune 'The Washington Post', and all the children marched across the hall towards the piano, swung right and went all around the hall, arms swinging, feet stamping and we singing 'All of a sudden a lump of black puddin' came rollin' down the stairs,' which the teachers didn't like one bit.

The leader would continue to march us round the hall until we were almost back to where we had started from. At this point the teacher would blow a shrill blast on a whistle and she'd march backwards in front of the leader over towards the far wall, and as soon as the leader reached the wall another blast on the whistle would make her turn sharp right over again to the opposite wall. This snake-like procession would continue until the leader had reached the top of the hall near the platform.

There, immobile as a statue upon a dais, stood an elderly woman with grey hair brought back behind her head in a bun and her hands joined loosely in front of her. She always wore a tweed skirt and twinset, woollen stockings and brogue shoes. We called her Lady Guinness.

As soon as the children were assembled and a hush had fallen on the hall, Lady Guinness shot into life. She raised her right hand to her shoulder, gave three beats to the bar and we all burst into a lusty

<blockquote>
Good evening to you
Good evening to you
Good evening Lady Guinness
Good evening to you.
</blockquote>

After a slight pause she raised her hand again and conducted us into

<blockquote>
We are children, good children we come here to play,
To sing and be happy and cheerful and gay,
And dear Lady Guinness, her heart is so good,
She helps us poor children to do as we should.
</blockquote>

These greetings and felicitations over, there would follow a few short announcements about the day's activities, but before we dispersed to our various rooms the highlight of the day, and the reason why most of us were there in the first place, was performed. This was the distribution of the buns and the tin mugs of shell cocoa. Some poor children really looked forward to these and the way they wired into the buns showed just how hungry they were. The buns were studded with sultanas and currants, which I thought looked like dead flies, and the tops were shiny and sticky. Some of the kids brought paper bags and collected buns from those like myself who couldn't stand the fruit. Even half-eaten buns were swooped up and they were brought home for tea. The shell cocoa in the tin mugs used to scald the lips off us, because it was already milked and sugared in the huge kettles and jugs. Sometimes the cocoa was quite undrinkable.

At that time in Dublin, shell cocoa was bought by a great many poor people who couldn't afford cocoa powder. My mother bought it on a number of occasions, but she gave it up because we wouldn't drink it. Years later I read in the papers that shell cocoa was highly toxic and quite unfit for human consumption.

After the bun and cocoa had revived our flagging spirits we would rush off to the different classrooms depending on our age-group. We were divided into infants, juniors and seniors, and our activities included knitting, sewing on machines, basket-making, dancing, drill, playing games or reading in the library. Anyone who had brought a toddler was expected to stay with it in the nursery, which wasn't very popular, and as soon as the teacher wasn't looking the toddler was abandoned, until its screams brought its predicament to the attention

Bayno, Iveagh Playcentre, Bull Alley. Opened 1915

of the teacher. Then the hunt would start for the escapee to find out which class she was in and we would all join in the confusion until she was caught. It was hilarious, but too much of that behaviour and you were barred for life.

Every year the children in the Bayno were treated to a Christmas Party. Admittance was by ticket only, and these were reserved for the regular attenders. One year, my school pal, Annie Molloy from the Coombe, got two tickets and invited me along. I had never been to a party in my life so I was quite excited. The world and Garrett Reilly were there, and like everyone else I had my brown paper bag to collect some of the goodies for my mother. Instead of buns and shell cocoa we got lovely bottles of lemonade and skinny bars of Cadbury's chocolate, Jacob's biscuits of every variety, balloons, paper hats, streamers and paper blow-outs, bags of sweets and fizz-bags.

The goodies were being swiped right, left and centre and it was all I could do to hold onto my presents and the biscuits, which got all mashed up in the bag. Then the blinds were pulled down and the Charlie Chaplin films started, and we couldn't stop laughing because as well as the films being funny themselves, they kept coming out upside down or the projector would break down, small kids were roaring and bawling, fights broke out and no one would sit down. It was a relief when it was all over, but it was great gas all the same and I'll never forget that skinny bar of Cadbury's chocolate — it was delicious.

Sadly the Bayno is no more. It lasted fifty years and during that time it served its purpose well. It was probably the first after-school-care institution in the country and there can be no doubt that the children who attended it really enjoyed themselves. With the passage of time the tenements in the surrounding streets were depleted and demolished, the families were banished to the outskirts of the city to housing estates where there were no facilities whatsoever and attendances at the Bayno dropped to an all-time low. In one way the families were better off, in that they had proper houses with toilets, water on tap, bedrooms and gardens, but their relations, friends and neighbours weren't there, the shops, schools, churches, the dealers, pawn shops, hustle, bustle, atmosphere, bumping into people they knew all their lives, the cinemas, theatres, dance-halls, factories, yards and offices, the security of community life was gone. The Corporation housing schemes gave them houses, but it stripped away the fabric of their lives.

The Bayno finally closed its doors at the end of September 1959, having been open for a total of 10,052 days with attendances of 7,820,520 children between the ages of three and fourteen years of age. Lord Iveagh's wish on the opening day that the children would ever look back on the happy days spent there have been realised, for any time I happen to meet my old school pals and we talk about the old times, someone is invariably sure to say, 'Will you ever forget the day in the Bayno when....

Smells and Pests

I think, I think, I smell a stink,
I think, I think, I do,
I think, I think, I smell a stink,
And I think it's off of **you**.

When we wanted to play chasing we would stand in a row and one of us would recite the jingle, pointing at each child in turn. Who ever was **you** was then 'on it'.

But the smells of Pimlico couldn't be chased away. There was no escape from them and they were powerful and varied. There were the smells we had to endure in the rooms from the slop-buckets under the beds, the stench from the outdoor lavatories in the back yards which were seldom cleaned, Keeffes the knackers in Newmarket, Hird's hide and skin yard in Marrowbone Lane, the skin yard in Catherine's Lane, the pig-sties, stables and cowsheds, Watkin's Brewery in Ardee Street, Guinness's Brewery in Belview and all the malt-houses which abounded on all sides.

Barrels steaming with mash from Power's Distillery in John's Lane would come trundling down the street, belching out obnoxious fumes. This was sold as animal feed and after eating it, it was no wonder that the animals stank.

The countrymen who came with the turf and vegetables on Saturdays would go round the stables and barns when their carts were empty. They would make their homeward journey filled to the brim with manure. A full cartload cost five shillings from Chrissie Masterson or Docko in Braithewaite Street, or from Hoppy Lawlor in Marrowbone Lane.

All the smells weren't there in the same concentration all the time. Each day one or two would outsmell all the others. It depended on whatever industrial process was being carried out or whatever way the wind was blowing or whether the sewers were blocked.

Dead horses passed regularly down the street in open horse-drawn carts, covered by bloodstained tarpaulins, on their way to Keeffes. Sometimes they weren't properly covered and we could see their legs sticking up stiffly or their eyes staring in a deadly gaze. Everyone around agreed that the most obnoxious smell came from Keeffes the knackers. At times it used make us feel sick and often the nuns in school would have to close the windows to stop themselves from keeling over.

God only knows what damage was being done to our lungs, yet in spite of their dislike for it many of the old neighbours would say that it was a very healthy smell. It didn't kill them anyway.

The old people also said that the smell of boiling tar was a great cure for whooping-cough and many a poor unfortunate child was suspended over the tar-barrel and nearly smothered with the fumes, heaving and gasping for breath between bouts of coughing.

The men who worked in the skin yards or in Keeffes stank to high heaven. Johnny Douglas, who lived opposite us, would have to strip off and wash himself under the tap in the back yard when he came home from work. Although the workers wore rubber boots and aprons over their clothes, the blood and smells from the animals' insides penetrated everything. Workers who didn't live in the area would have to footslog it home from work because they wouldn't be allowed on public transport.

But not all the smells were bad. I loved the smell of Guinness's and the malt-house in Meath Place. The tiny windows in the malt-houses were down almost at pavement level with iron bars on the outside. On the way home from school I would peep through the bars if the light was on and see the workmen walking about in the barley in their bare feet. It seemed to me most unhygienic and when I said so to my mother she said, 'Well, wouldn't it be worse if they had their boots on.'

Another of my favourite smells was Mr Russell's dairy across the road in Marrowbone Lane. I would be sent with the milk-can for a ha'port of loose milk or buttermilk for the mashed potatoes. We never used milk in tea, only sweetened condensed tinned milk which had a notice in big type, UNFIT FOR BABIES. This stern warning didn't prevent the mothers from dipping the babies' rubber soothers into the tin and scooping up a big dollop which went straight into the babies' bawling mouths. Anything for a quiet life.

Mick Russell's dairy was lovely and clean with a beautiful milky, buttery, dairy smell. The counter top was a long slab of white marble on which stood three enormous white delft vats with pictures of blue cows contentedly grazing in fields of blue grass. Milk, Cream and Buttermilk was written on the outsides. Hanging over the edge into each vat was a tin tilly and draped over each vat was a piece of snow-white muslin to keep out dust and flies. On the floor against the wall stood huge milk churns which Mick would put in his milk-cart for delivery around the streets every morning and evening.

The smells had their camp-followers — the millions of flies, bluebottles and multitudinous insects against which we waged a relentless war. Fly-paper, which was sold in a roll like film, was hung up on ceilings to catch the flies. It had a sticky surface and when covered with dead flies and bluebottles it looked quite disgusting. My mother couldn't stand it so she kept herself fighting fit with a rolled-up newspaper swiping at the winged prey.

One smell will haunt me all my life and that is the very distinctive smell of bugs. These were flat, red-brown creepy-crawlies that lived behind the wallpaper. The houses were very old and the walls were a mixture of plaster and hair, held together with layers and layers of wallpaper. It was almost disastrous to try to remove the wallpaper for repapering because in doing so lumps of plaster and hair fell off leaving the walls all pockmarked.

Granny's room in No 35 Pimlico was infested with these pests. My brother Paddy lived with her and Uncle Paddy and Uncle Christy, which was an advantage to them and to us. He did all sorts of chores for them and it meant one less in the bed for us. A population explosion had taken place among the bugs and my mother decided it was about time to make an all-out assault on them. Powdered DDT had become very popular in the war against flies and insects, so a couple of boxes of this were bought. My brothers and I were recruited, a big fire was laid down in the grate, the beds were pulled into the centre of the room and the small pieces of furniture were put on the landing. We were armed with shovels and sweeping brushes. The war began.

As the wallpaper was pulled off the wall the bugs scampered in their thousands. My mother and Sean then swept the bugs down onto the shovels held by Stephen and Paddy, who then rushed to the blazing fire and threw them in. As I was only seven years old my job was to dance on the ones running about the floor. The bugs' bodies snapped, crackled and popped in the flames and the smell of roasting bugs will remain in my nostrils forever.

My mother's anti-bug campaign was thorough and effective. The DDT was thrown around like snuff at a wake and every day for a week she repeated the powdered dose. Christy Smith the handyman bunged up the holes with plaster, and when my mother was finally satisfied that not one bug was left alive she put up new wallpaper. I haven't seen a bug since.

However, another torture beset us during the war years when turf was the only fuel available. The city was plagued with hoppers. When we got out of bed in the morning our bodies were tattooed with red spots and the sheets were covered with blood from the jumping bloodsuckers.

Sir Charles Cameron, City Medical Officer, ready for action

The DDT was again brought into action. My mother dusted it between the blankets and the sheets, all over the tick mattress, in the pillow cases, under the beds and all round the edges of the floorboards. When we got into bed we were covered with it. It killed the flies and the flypaper became redundant. What we didn't know until years later was that it wasn't doing us any good either and in fact it may have been more harmful to us than the flies and insects were.

One of our favourite pastimes during the summer months when the air was ahum with the buzzing of flies was to stand outside the tenements watching the flies alight upon the walls. We had been assured by one of our pals who had read it in the Reader's Digest that before a fly flew forward it flew backwards an eighth of an inch.

Armed with this piece of indisputable scientific knowledge we lay in wait for our quarry. We would slowly and carefully move our cupped hands along the wall behind the victim and with a quick flash of the wrist capture it in the palm of the hand. We would then remove the wings and either put the helpless fly in a matchbox or into a spider's web and watch it being devoured.

Our parents encouraged us in this particular pursuit which had its origins way back in the year 1911. My mother well remembered the summer of that year for a number of reasons. In August there was a strike in Jacob's where she worked and many of the strikers were injured in a baton charge by the police in Parliament Street. There was an unusually warm summer and autumn. A serious epidemic of infantile diarrhoea broke out and there was an immense number of flies around.

Altogether 643 deaths from diarrhoeal diseases were recorded, the main victims being the children who lived in the insanitary tenements. Flies seemed to be everywhere and a direct connection between the flies and the high death-rate was established. In the newspapers there was a call for action against what Sir Charles Cameron, the Chief Medical Officer, called the 'disease distributor'. He recommended the use of fly-paper and a solution of formalin in six parts water placed in saucers. The shops were running out of Keating's Powder whicn was being puffed and dusted in every direction. The *Evening Herald* of 19 August advised that 'practically the only thing a fly or a mosquito is afraid of is an electric fan'. As the people most affected by the flies hadn't even proper homes, never mind electricity or fans, this piece of advice sounded as if it came from the Marie Antoinette stable.

Finally Sir Charles Cameron hit upon the idea of purchasing the flies as an incentive to the people to wage war upon them. His suggestion was adopted and 126,000 flies were bought, the vendors being young boys who entered into the battle with great gusto. Sir Charles admitted that the idea occurred to him late in the year and had the purchase of the flies commenced earlier millions would have been procured. His proposal was much ridiculed and became the subject of several kinds of picture postcards.

However, Sir Charles started us off on a pastime which occupied Dublin children for many a long hot summer until improved housing, proper sanitation and the introduction of deadly fly-killers reduced the disease distributor to manageable numbers.

Rats and mice shared our living quarters in large numbers also. At night time the mice could be heard nibbling away at the floorboards and wallpaper and scuttling in and out of the cupboards. Worst of all they destroyed our food and many a time the only bit we might have in the cupboard would have to be thrown out. Mousetraps were absolutely essential pieces of household equipment but controlling the rats was a much harder task. Their nests were outside in the yards and laying poison was too expensive and dangerous with so many small children and domestic animals about. The stables, skinyards and pigsties were their breeding grounds and the grain in the area drew them like a magnet. Trying to get rid of the rodents was like trying to empty the ocean with a spoon.

One day, when I was quite young, a blockage occurred in the sewers at the top of the Coombe. As the gases built up, the manhole covers in the middle of the road in Pimlico blew off, one after the other, and the sewage rose up and spilled all over the street. Hundreds of sewer rats escaped with the liquid effluent and they scampered everywhere. Everyone old enough remembers their appearance, their long bodies and tails and their coarse bristly hair. They ran into the open halls of the tenements, up the stairs and out into the yards causing terror and confusion. This was considered the height of bad luck — plague and pestilence were predicted, not to mention the end of the world.

Customs, Superstitions and Cures

> Bright yellow, red and orange,
> The leaves come down in hosts;
> The trees are Indian princes,
> And soon will turn to ghosts.

Stephen learned the words of Allingham's poem in school and he used to sing it to the tune of 'Let him go, let him tarry', which was a way we had of remembering the words of poetry because it made it easier. On the way to school in late September the words always came to mind as we scattered the fallen leaves from the trees in the Swingin' Boats as they thickly lined the footpaths in Pimlico and Meath Place.

Autumn was my favourite time of year. A wonderful change of colour and atmosphere came over the street which was a reflection of the leaves still remaining on the trees and those which had fallen to the ground. It was great to run through them and hear the lovely swishy crunchy sound and to kick heaps of them into the air or to watch them being whipped up into swirling circles by the fairy winds.

The falling leaves, the fairy winds, the slight autumnal nip in the air, the closing in of the evenings and the anticipated excitement of Halloweve acted on our senses like a sorcerer's potion. Forces beyond our understanding were at work, changing our environment and changing our attitudes and moods. We became introspective, superstitious and much more God-fearing. When Billy-with-the-lamplight came around with his long rod to light the gas street-lamps we knew by instinct that it was story-telling time again.

In the evening after tea we would gather in groups as dusk descended and sit on a low window-sill or at the edge of the footpath up the Square, or better still, at the bottom of the stairs in one of the tenement halls, the doors of which were always open. We would huddle together for warmth and security, the closeness helping us to cope with the fear we were about to generate. When Billy-with-the-lamplight made his appearance we would all start chanting:

> Billy with the lamplight,
> Billy the fool,
> Billy with the wooden leg,
> Wouldn't go to school.

For some reason which we could never understand, this used to annoy him intensely and instead of ignoring us he would give chase, which was exactly what we wanted, for while he was hot-foot after some of us the rest were taking his ladder and hiding it behind one of the cottages in the Square.

The flickering gas light created shadows which set the scene for our story-telling. We had been raised on boogey-men, spirits, ghosts, devils and demons and our fertile imaginations ran riot. We vied with one another to see who could tell the most hair-raising ghost story, and we never tired of hearing the same ones again and again, because someone was always sure to give them a different twist. We terrified the living daylights out of ourselves, enjoying every minute of horror, and spent sleepless nights sweating in our beds, hearts thumping out through our ribs, wishing for daylight to bring blessed relief from the agony.

For dramatic effect, the stories were always told in a low voice, until just at the end whoever was telling the story would suddenly bawl out the last few words and jump up. This action, although not altogether unexpected, would scatter the rest of us in all directions, screaming as if all the devils in hell were after us.

When I was only about six years old and we were living in No 33 Pimlico, I first became aware of the Man With The Heavy Foot who had apparently been haunting the house for many years. He would come in the small hours of the morning and slowly thump, thump into the hall and out into the back yard, then back into the hall and slowly thump, thump up the wooden stairs, pause for a while at the top of the house and thump, thump down again. Sometimes we would hear chains rattling as if he was dragging something, and worst of all, he would occasionally give three loud knocks on a door which took his fancy. We would all lie awake frightened to death but no one ever went out to see who it was, and for very good reason.

The story goes that many years before, when my mother was only a young girl, the Man With The Heavy Foot was paying his customary visit and had reached the top of the house when Christy Smith's father, who was a fine, big lump of a man in the whole of his health, decided to put a stop to yer man's gallop, but when he got to the top of the house there was no one there. He fell into a decline from then on and within three weeks he was stone dead. So it was no wonder that nobody would get up out of the sack to investigate. In the light of day, after one of the Man's visits, my mother would try to dispel our fears by saying it was only an oul' tramp, but at night when He was on His rounds, she was just as terrified as the rest of us.

The Clutchin' Hand and the Hairy Hand were two regular feelers on the dark stairways. Their visitations usually followed a day spent in the picture house looking at some horror film. The stairs in the tenements were very rickety and uneven, so it was in the interest of safety to hold onto the banisters when going up or coming down in the dark. We would be only about half way up when one of the Hands would strike, coming down on the hand on the banisters, and depending on whichever Hand it was it was cold and clammy or hairy to the touch. Many a neck was nearly broken trying to take the stairs in one jump. Whenever anyone was telling their experiences of the Hands one of us was sure to feel their touch on the back of the neck and we'd again scatter screaming in terror.

One of my greatest fears was of the Banshee, because her mournful wailings always heralded someone's death and I was terrified it would be my mother's. The Banshee's caterwauling would always start after midnight and she could be at it up to three or four o'clock in the morning. She would position herself over at the blank wall beside Mrs Doyle's, just opposite my granny's window, and as soon as she'd start my heart would pound so loudly that I could hear it through my ear on the pillow. She would come three nights on the trot, just to make sure that the person she had come for got good warning. My mother used to say that it was only a cat, but still and all, there were times when even she admitted that no earthly creature could make such a spine-chilling sound. It wasn't lucky to get up to have a look at her, but those who had seen her described her as a little small woman, with long flowing fair hair which reached down to the ground, and as she wailed her song of death she ran her rack-comb through it. If you were unfortunate enough to be abroad when she was on duty you had to be sure to say, 'Good night, ma'am,' when passing her by or she would throw the rack after you and if it struck you, you were a gonner.

The holy pictures on the walls were another source of terror. In the middle of the night they used to communicate with each other by tap-tapping on the glass in the frames. St Patrick and

Outdoor altar

Johnson collection/RTE

Our Lady of Perpetual Succour were forever sending cryptic messages across the room and waking me up and then the death-watch beetles would begin their tick-ticking under the bed and gallons of sweat would pour from my glands. I would pull the clothes over my head and thank God that I slept in the middle of the five of us in the bed.

On Halloweve night we would all dress-up in the strangest outfits and blacken our faces. Armed with handbags and paper bags we would set off on a begging mission for the Halloweve party. The streets were always thronged with hundreds of other children doing the same thing, and when one gang encountered another we would stop to exchange experiences and to boast about the amount of money, fruit and nuts we had collected. The people were extremely generous and we were never refused a contribution towards the feast. We had the greatest fun frightening the lives out of each other going up the dark stairs of the tenements, particularly in the 'trickin' halls' in School Street and Earl Street. These were tenements which shared a common yard so that it was possible to go into one house, go out the yard and come back through another house. The most frightening thing to do on Halloweve night was to look in a mirror at twelve o'clock because if you did you saw the devil looking over your shoulder.

On All Soul's Night every one of our dead relatives came to visit us. They would be seen sitting on chairs, or standing motionless at the end of the bed, looking none the worse for having been buried six feet under the sod, many of them for donkey's years. When I was very young my mother used light a big white wax candle when we were going to bed so that the wandering spirits of all our relations could find their way home.

The fountain at the side wall of our house was haunted because this was where the old manor house stood. Some people were known to have seen a tall figure in flowing robes standing on the steps of the fountain, and as soon as they got beside it the figure would disappear through the wall into our yard. He was supposed to be one of the monks from the old Abbey of St Thomas.

Maggie Hanbury lived up the Long Entry and I don't know how many times she saw a woman ghost all dressed in white, with red hair, who appeared from nowhere as soon as you got as far as Mick Murphy's door, and she'd float silently along with you until you reached either Earl Street or Pimlico, depending on the way you were going.

We all knew that Watkin's Brewery and the Nurses' Home in Ardee Street were haunted, but they seemed to share the same ghost. My mother said that there was a poltergeist in the malt-house when she was young and Fr J. Kelly, who was the parish priest in Meath Street at the time, sent a young curate out to banish the spirit. Strange happenings, noises of things being thrown about, chains rattling, doors banging and unmerciful screams in the underground passages were heard by the night-workers, who became afraid and refused to go to work. So the young priest from Meath Street arrived. He had lovely jet-black hair and a fresh complexion when he went into the malt-house, but after staying there alone for three days and three nights he emerged a wizened old man with hair as white as the driven snow.

There was nothing I liked better on a cold, dark Saturday night, than to be taken up to granny's room and put into her bed at the far wall opposite the fireplace. Granny's brothers, Uncles Paddy and Christy, would come home with a few cronies from the pub, all well-oiled, and they'd spend the night either singing and playing music or telling stories. My mother would play her concertina or the mouth organ and Tommy McDonnell would play his melodeon. Granny was a lovely singer and Uncle Paddy was a great storyteller.

My mother would have a coddle or a few pigs' feet all ready for the night's entertainment and a big blazing fire laid down. On these occasions the oil lamp was never lit. The only light came from the dancing flames of the fire. Everyone would settle themselves around the fireplace, which was at an angle in the wall, on stools, forms and kitchen chairs. The glass tumblers and the corkscrew were taken down off the dresser and granny's long-handled enamel ladle would scoop up great big dollops of coddle from the black iron skillet pot, or a steaming dish of pigs' feet would be plonked in the middle of the deal table.

I would watch the action from the bed, the flames from the fire visible only now and again when someone moved to pick up a glass or to poke a piece of paper into the fire to light a pipe. The stories Uncle Paddy told were very long and involved and usually I fell asleep before the end. Strange things were always happening to him and Uncle Christy on their many journeys out to 'do the bona fide' after the city pubs had closed. These trips out into the countryside to such far-away places as the Cuckoo's Nest in Walkinstown, The Fox Covert in Tallaght, the Lamb Doyle's in Ticknock, the Dead Man's near Lucan, the Wren's Nest in the Strawberry Beds or the Morgue in Templeogue were taken in an ass and cart or a pony and trap. Many of the neighbours around owned these so there was never any transport problem.

From travelling to do the bona fide so often, the animals knew their way there and back no matter which country road was taken, and they were always given their heads, which was just as well because their cargo was usually 'blotto' on the way out and unconscious with drink on the way back. Their stories of strange happenings on the journey were hair-raising, but my mother, who was a terrible cynic, would always attribute their supernatural experiences to the amount of porter they'd consumed. Invariably, it was the ass or the pony that would first sense that something was wrong and would come to such a sudden halt on the roadway that the passengers on board would be pitched headlong out of the cart or trap. This jolted them into a sufficient degree of consciousness to enable them to make an intelligent assessment of whatever phenomenon was about to appear.

The apparitions always occurred when they were passing a graveyard, a ruined castle, ancient church or old house, or at a spot where some terrible atrocity had taken place. Their imaginations ran away with them as they recounted stories of the Pooka, the Large Black Dog, The Headless Man on the Headless Horse, the Wailing Woman in White or the Ghostly Coach and Four.

Whenever anyone died at home, somebody was sure to meet their ghost on the landing or out the back yard late at night, particularly if the person had been found dead after a few days had passed without them being seen. This happened quite a lot to old people who lived alone and kept to themselves. Poor Biddy Minogue, an old woman who had a huxter shop opposite us at the corner of Marrowbone Lane, was dead for three weeks before anyone found her. Someone with good smellers happened to be standing at her door one day and, following enquiries, informed the police in Newmarket. Because she wasn't in the habit of opening every day, nobody noticed that Biddy wasn't around.

We were never in too much of a hurry to bury our dead and I well remember wakes going on for as long as three nights. Although there was genuine sadness whenever anyone passed away, the wakes were lively affairs. The neighbours were very supportive of the relatives and they'd take over the running of the wake. The news of the death would spread round the street like wildfire and if the deceased was a member of a family long resident in the street, all the blinds in every house were pulled down or the curtains were closed. Our Protestant neighbours observed this custom too, as a mark of respect. The blinds and curtains would remain thus until after the funeral, and even then many neighbours would open them only half way until the day after the funeral.

When the corpse was in the house a death card was nailed to the front door giving all particulars such as the name, age and the date of death, ending with RIP. All around the card a piece of black crepe was arranged which indicated that the corpse was in the house. When a person died elsewhere, only the card was put on the door. Most people occupied only one room in the tenements, and when anyone died at home one of the neighbours would lend their room for the wake. A couple of women would wash and lay out the corpse, whether it was male or female. The usual attire was a habit of the 'ornamental brown' with a big emblem displaying the initials IHS. Sometimes there was also a bleeding heart on the emblem. Members of some sodalities had their own particular coloured habits such as the Children of Mary, which was blue with a white veil.

The corpse was laid out on a white sheet on the bed until the coffin arrived and if there was nowhere else to put the coffin it stayed on the bed, because not every family had a table and some of them hadn't even beds. Tallow candles were lit on either side of the corpse and a saucer of snuff and a dish of holy water were placed on a table at the foot of the corpse. Rosary beads were entwined around the joined hands with the cross propped-up between the thumbs and forefingers. Occasionally two pennies were put on the eyes to keep them shut until rigor mortis set in.

Towards evening the mourners would arrive carrying grey bags of porter or black bags of stout or maybe something a little stronger. According to custom, the relatives would stay in the room with the corpse along with the women who were keeping the vigil. Throughout the night they would take it in turns to go to bed and there were often so many in the bed that instead of lying lengthways they'd have to lie across the bed. As well as keeping the vigil, these women had to keep their eyes to business, noting who came and what they brought, as this was a most important piece of information for the relatives. It was considered the essence of badness not to pay respects to the dead, and failure to do so would be held against a person for ever.

Some people were professional wake-goers and every evening they would scrutinise the *Herald* and *Mail* death notices and, whether they knew the corpse or not, they'd call up to the house to utter their condolences. Many of these were musicians for whom wakes were a way of life, so to speak. If the wake was to their liking they would see it out to the end and if not they would find another. In this way they were kept in food and drink for several days at a time.

Wakes were a great source of entertainment for us children and, like the musicians, if we saw a crepe on a door we'd make it our business to call in to see the corpse that night. There was usually a drop of lemonade and a few biscuits to be had if the relatives knew us, but sometimes we'd barge into a wake where we weren't known just for fun. Going up the stairs of a tenement house in the dark to see a corpse was great gas. No one wanted to be first and no one wanted to be last especially on the way down after being in the presence of death. We'd get wedged on the landings and stairways, pulling the clothes off each other trying to stay in the middle, and the racket we'd kick up would nearly wake the dead. We all saw something on the corpse move, an eye, the mouth, a finger, the head and we even saw some of them breathing.

The lack of variety in our diet left us vulnerable to all kinds of ailments within and without. In winter time our fingers, toes and heels swelled up and became red and itchy. After a while of tearing and scratching, the skin would break and if not looked after, would sometimes fester. These were chilblains caused by a lack of calcium and aggravated by the cold. As soon as the heat got at them they went mad throbbing, a condition we called bealing. The cure we had for them was to soak them in our own pee! Needless to remark, it didn't work.

When I went for a medical examination before starting in Jacob's, Dr Bewley gazed in horror at the condition of my feet, legs and hands. 'Calcium, child, calcium is what you need. Get your mother to buy you plenty of cheese and milk and they'll be gone in a week.' They were too, and I've never had them since.

Every so often a plague of warts would break out and our hands would resemble the great canyons of the Rocky Mountains. To get rid of these, the best thing was the fasting spittle, applied liberally, or to bury a piece of bacon in the back yard or a dose of ink from the school-desk ink-well. I can vouch for the fasting spittle because it worked for me.

We were forever getting cuts from falls, sharp instruments, broken glass and razor blades and as our epidermis was none too clean, the cuts usually ended up becoming septic. These were 'let go' with needles and pins and covered over with sticking plaster or else given a rub of zam-buk ointment. Anything big like a boil or a carbuncle got a good slap of the scalding poultice, made from boiling water and flakemeal, and if that didn't make you hop nothing would.

Styes spread among us like wildfire and were the very divil to get rid of. Bathing the eye with cold tea was recommended or the rub of a gold ring on the affected eye. Maybe we didn't have the faith, because in the end my mother would have to consult Mr Mushat, the chemist in Francis Street, who had a cure for everything from flat feet to alopecia.

The 'bronicals' (chest trouble) and sore throats were left in the capable hands of St Blaise. Each year on his feast day in February there wouldn't be a bit of red flannel to be had in Duffy's or Frawley's, but the dealers outside Adam and Eve's on Merchant's Quay had plenty as well as the candles and the olive oil. Diphtheria and whooping cough were such killers that our parents felt the need for divine intervention to back up the vapours of the tar-barrel.

Foot ailments were very common among the adults but the complaints originated in childhood, caused mainly by the wearing of second-hand shoes and boots, which were either too big or too small. Bunions, corns, welts, ingrown toenails and fallen arches were presented daily to Mr Mushat for cure and some of the 'understandings' were in a terrible state. A favourite pastime of the corn sufferers was to spend painful evenings after a footbath, scraping and paring away at the corn with penknives, pins, pointed scissors and Max-Smile razor blades. My mother's toes were tattooed with corn plasters, and every pair of shoes she bought had to have two large holes cut at the big-toe side to give the bunions a bit of freedom and release the pressure.

Mushat's Chemist Shop, Francis Street and list of KK cures, 1923-1967

Animals and Birds

Wednesdays and Thursdays were like fair-days in Pimlico. The cattle drovers, wielding ashplants, hunched the cows, sheep and pigs, beating them mercilessly from the Cattle Market to the slaughter-houses or to the various yards in the area. They also travelled in the opposite direction, going to the Cattle Market for sale.

The chaos created was hilarious when drovers travelling in opposite directions met. One of the worst places for this — or the best, depending on whether you were a drover or an onlooker — was the junction of Thomas Court, Earl Street, School Street and the Bawn.

It was a pantomime watching the antics of the drovers as they tried to extricate their animals from the herds. Everybody joined in the act, which wasn't at all helpful as even the drovers weren't sure who owned which animal unless one had all sheep and the other had cows or pigs. All traffic would come to a standstill as animals, drovers, dogs and helpers rushed in all directions. Shooing, waving, cursing, and animal noises added to the general air of confusion and entertainment.

All the while they waved their arms, the drovers roared 'How-up, how-up.' They brought their ashplants down with force on every part of the animals' bodies inflicting unnecessary pain and terror.

We were terrified of the animals, especially the cattle, because to us every cow without udders was a bull. As soon as we heard the bellowings, grunts or bleatings we would scatter into the nearest tenement or up the Long Entry, screaming as if all the animals of the jungle were after us. Older boys displayed acts of bravery, motivated by divilment, by rushing in among the animals from the front and causing them to change direction. Like the toreros of Spain they hoped to perform some skilled side-stepping and be chased by the cattle, but the chasing was usually done by the drover, who found his job difficult enough without being provoked by our fun-seeking heroes.

Milking-cows were a pitiful sight, some of them hardly able to walk with milk pouring from their swollen udders. Many a time they would have to be milked by one of the neighbours in the street before they were able to proceed on their tortured way.

The animals were always running into the tenement halls, and on one memorable occasion when we were living in No 33 Pimlico a cow ran in and got jammed in the hallway between our door and Mrs Douglas's, who lived opposite.

One of the drovers ran into the yard of No 34 and climbed over the wall. He kept hitting the cow on the head while the other drover was behind, yanking its tail and heaving backwards. Crowds gathered in the hall and in the yard, yelling words of encouragement and good advice. The cow scuttered all over the hall and the drover kept slipping and sliding. My mother and I were terrified inside the room convinced that the door and the cow were going to burst in.

Eventually Johnny Douglas, who drove a horse and cart for Keeffes the knackers, opened his door to allow the poor cow room to manoeuvre. As soon as the cow felt the bit of leeway it went wild into the room, knocking over chairs and kicking in every direction. What was even worse it left its watery message all over the lino.

The smell was terrible and the destruction incredible. When the cow finally reached the freedom of the street it careered and charged in every direction. The drovers were just as wild with temper because while they were trying to disengage the cow in the hall the rest of the herd had wandered off in all directions, aided and abetted by the children who couldn't resist contributing to the fun.

In winter time, when the roads were covered with ice and frost, the horses provided us with more drama. They slipped and skidded all over the roads and the cobble-stones. Some drivers carried a supply of sacks, and with the help of many willing hands would try to get them into position under the horse's feet and belly. It was a pitiful sight to see a horse down, trembling with fear and hurt, froth oozing from its mouth, and its eyes rolling in its head. Some carters were cruel and would whip the horse to get it to try struggling to its feet. Buckets of cold ashes and cinders would be rushed out of the houses and scattered under the hoofs. We viewed these scenes with a mixture of excitement and sadness, torn between the love of the drama and concern for the horse's plight.

A runway horse was as good as a cowboy film. It was hair-raising to watch the driver bent backwards like a rodeo rider straining and pulling on the reins, yelling 'Hike, ho-there, ho-there,' at the top of his voice, as the animal bolted up Pimlico. People and traffic would scatter. It often took the length of Pimlico before a horse could be brought to a halt and sometimes this was only achieved by the bravery of some man courageous enough to rush the horse and hold onto its head for long enough.

One poor horse had a sad ending. It was owned by Tucker Gilson who lived up in School Street. Tucker's horse was a big black stallion which he grazed up in Mooney's field at the Back-of-the-Pipes. It was a wild and stubborn beast and the only one who had any control over it was Doco, who knew all that was to be known about horses and all other animals besides.

This day Tucker was in having his dinner and the stallion was yoked up under a dray. Just outside the house was an air-raid shelter, the door of which was made of slats of wood. Tucker tied the stallion to the door with a halter to keep him from roaming off.

The horse's form was legendary, and didn't some bright spark decide to indulge his idea of fun. He gave the stallion a right belt up the rear end, which sent it leaping sky-high. It broke the halter, galloped down School Street around the Bawn into Pimlico. The chase was on as the animal careered from one side of the road to the other and women screamed and endangered their lives as they tried to drag young children in off the roadway. The braves chasing the horse terrified it further until, blind with fear, it finally crashed into another air-raid shelter at the far end of Pimlico and did terrible injury to its head, neck and forelegs. The vet from Keeffes the knackers was sent for, and the poor unfortunate animal had to be put down and taken off in the knacker's cart by Johnny Douglas.

Pigeons were the bane of my mother's life and, God knows, Pimlico had its fair share of them. She considered them both dirty and unlucky and spent a great deal of her waking hours removing their shite from the windows and predicting disasters. Every time a pigeon landed on the window-sill, she would leap up from her butter box and rush to the window with her arms flailing about in all directions.

She was kept busy, for there were many pigeon fanciers in the street and round about. As well as those kept in captivity, the area was the natural habitat of hundreds of commoners, who were attracted there by the abundance of grain-spillage from the boats in Guinness's harbour and the storage houses for barley and wheat in Crane Lane and Forbes's Lane.

Right next door to us, in No 34, Duckser Healy kept a large pigeon loft in the back yard. A couple of doors down at the Swingin' Boats Whacker McCann had his loft. Down on the Banks, Powah, Joe and John Connor and Atsy Doran had their pigeons. Up in Marrowbone Lane, Dylser, Toucher and Hare Byrne, and Skatner and Johnboy Lannon had lofts and in Earl

Street and Ash Street lived the birds of Sparra Donegan and Crutchy Howard. All the lofts were in the back yards of tenement houses and those of the Marrowbone Lane fanciers were all in the one backyard. Competition, rivalry, robbery and rows were all part of the fanciers' world and from morning till night they never talked about anything else but breeding and racing pigeons.

Pigeons were as much a part of our domestic scene as cats, dogs, pigs, horses, cows, hens and cocks. Mice and rats were attracted to the lofts in great numbers because of the grain. Sometimes cats made the mistake of following the pigeons into the lofts, and when this happened all hell broke loose, with feathers, fur, cats and birds flying in all directions. To protect his pigeons at night, Duckser would put a board with holes up to the trap, because the rats not only ate the grain but would also eat the eggs and the youngsters.

It was possible to walk around the inside of Ducker's loft in which he kept a large variety of pigeons. Exchanges and sales went on between the fanciers, but Duckser's birds were so well trained that they wouldn't be a wet day gone until they'd be back. The loft was home-made out of bits and pieces but it had all the necessary requirements, including a landing platform and inside bars. It was divided into sections and was strewn with sawdust and had an ample supply of grain, grit, corn and water.

The birds were of every hue and variety — bellers, reds, red checks, bards, red mealies, blues, blue checks, blue white tips, blacks, checks, whites, white tips, and two tumblers who were called Patsy and Susie. The bellers were ferocious-looking with large wattles over their beaks and big eye-rings, and although I was surrounded by them all during my childhood, I was terrified of them.

When the pigeon racing came around there was always great excitement in the street. The races took place from the Esplanade between Collins' Barracks and the Liffey. All the Pimlico fanciers would be down on the Banks waiting for the flocks to appear. They knew precisely when, and as soon as the sky became filled with a cloud of pigeons they would send up the tumblers, whose antics of rolling and tumbling in a forward direction would throw the racers into a terrible state of confusion. This carry-on would bring down some of the racers to the waiting fanciers, who would then take off the rings or else bide their time before getting in touch with the pigeon club in the hope of getting a reward.

During the 'Emergency' my brother, Stephen, earned a tidy sum snaring pigeons and selling them to a rabbit firm in Denzille Lane, off Westland Row. They in turn exported them to England where apparently they were a wartime delicacy. Stephen was able to earn about thirty shillings a day, out of which he gave my mother twelve shillings. She was totally unaware of his bird-hunting expeditions, for although she disliked the pigeons she certainly wouldn't have approved of the cruelty of snaring.

So every morning Stephen and Joeboy Hensico from Thomas Court would set off, moryah, for the slaughterhouse to milk the poor cows before they met their doom. My mother would rise at a quarter to five to light the fire and get him a cup of tea and a cut of bread. She pitied him as he set off at half past five on his work of mercy to Smithfield Market.

Snaring pigeons was a pastime only indulged in by members of the male sex of all ages. The tools of the trade were a roll of fishing twine which could be bought in Doyle's shop beside Meath Street Chapel, a full pocket of grain which could be got for nothing at any of the granaries, a small piece of stick, fine pebbles the size of steeler marbles and a sling.

To make the sling Stephen cut a Y-shaped branch from a tree in the Swingin' Boats, peeled off the bark and pared it nice and neat for holding in the palm of the hand. About a quarter to a half inch from the top he cut a niche in the front on both sides. Two strips of rubber tubing, tied tightly with the fishing twine, were firmly secured in the niches and in the centre he tied the soft tongue of a boot. This was a deadly weapon.

Up the back of Guinness's was the favourite place for snaring because it was nice and quiet between working shifts and the pigeons were so plentiful they were asking to be caught. Here it wasn't necessary to use the sling. A loop was made with the twine and spread out on the ground in a circle, into which the grain was placed. Outside the circle more grain was placed in order to lure the pigeon into the snare. The piece of stick was tied to the other end of the twine and held in the closed fist and as soon as the poor unsuspecting pigeon stepped into the circle a good fast pull would tighten the snare around its legs.

There were times when either Stephen or Joeboy couldn't make the early morning shift and they would then have to go out to Blackrock to do the snaring because they didn't want anyone else in on the act. This is when they used the sling as they had to work fast. The tactic here was to encourage the pigeons to the ground with the grain and as soon as they became engrossed in the pecking their necks were broken with a sudden belt of a pebble fired with deadly, David-like accuracy from the sling. The captured birds were then stuffed inside their jackets, under their oxters. Stephen always returned from these hunting expeditions infested with pigeon fleas.

Pigeon Loft

The Bird Market in Bride Street was a favourite haunt of Uncle Paddy where he would spend many a happy hour on Sunday morning discussing with his old cronies the merits and otherwise of the various birds on view. He was very fond of our feathered friends and when I was very young he had a little bird called a redpoll which he bought in the Bird Market for sixpence. It had a lovely red spot on its forehead over its beak and a black spot under its chin. Uncle Paddy called it Redser and he was so attached to it that if he could have put it on a lead he would have taken it for walks.

Redser lived in a cage which the uncle used to hang up on a nail which was driven into the brick wall outside the right-hand window. Every morning during the fine weather Redser was suspended from his nail from where he could view all the goings-on in the street and the uncle would sit beside the open window keeping him company while watching points himself. The bird was great for twittering, which was greatly to the uncle's liking because this attracted the attention of passers-by who would then engage in long conversations with him as they stood on the footpath looking up at him looking down at them. Sometimes there'd be so many on the footpath that it was as though the uncle was addressing a meeting. The window wasn't very high up and as the uncle held court he leaned slightly forward with his head sticking out, wearing a hard hat which he never removed except when going to bed.

When the redpoll wasn't hanging outside he was decorating the wall inside the room much to granny's annoyance, for, like my mother, she couldn't abide birds or animals sharing the limited space with humans. One day when Uncle Paddy had gone out after he and granny had had words about Redser, granny hung the bird up on the wall outside the window to get it out of her sight. She forgot all about it and at some time during the day didn't a few go-boys notice that the bird was unattended and they quietly whipped it off the wall. There was only holy open desolation when Uncle Paddy returned and discovered that his bird had flown, cage and all, and he threatened to hang granny up on the wall in the hopes that someone would run away with her, but he doubted very much that anyone would run away with such an oul' hen.

He never ever bought another cage or bird, but he would sit at the open window watching the antics of the hundreds of crows, starlings, pigeons and seagulls as they squawked, squeaked, cawed and hooted to beat the band. The starlings nested in their thousands in the eaves of the houses in Marrowbone Lane, especially in the vicinity of the Widows' Home. Here, they would congregate on the roofs during the day, creating the most awful din, swooping suddenly in a dark wing-flapping cloud down the narrow street, settling just as suddenly before repeating the same sudden flight.

The jackdaws and crows nested in the high trees in the Swingin' Boats and their rasping caw-cawing and bustling early-morning activity was a great help in getting the brewery men out of their beds in the morning for the early shift. To add to the confusion, Julia Hennessy's cock would start its cockadoodleooing at about four o'clock in the morning and it would even do it sometimes during the day when it had no call or business to do so, which my mother said was the height of bad luck.

Mrs O'Neill, wife of the Scab O'Neill, who went to work during the transport workers' strike of 1935, heavily guarded by policemen right from the door of No 34, kept a flock of chickens in a hen-run in the back yard. We were forever letting them escape and they'd run into the communal lavatory or up the stairs and into the different rooms or out the hall door and down the street in every direction. We'd have great fun pretending to catch them for her when all the time we'd be shooing them out onto the road. The dogs and the cats never paid a blind bit of attention to them as they waddled quite unconcernedly all about, pecking at every bit of grain and grit blown out from the pigeon lofts.

Our nicest birds were the beautiful white swans and their cygnets who used sail so gracefully upon the waters of the canal and the smaller waterhens and their chicks who lived in the reeds and vegetation beside the canal banks between the Iron Bridge and Rialto Bridge.

The swans didn't like us to get too close with our fishing nets when we went catching pinkeens, and they'd hiss and beat their wings to warn us off. Sometimes the swans would suddenly take to the air and fly right the way up along the canal with a fierce, loud flapping of wings, which was magnificent to watch.

All that is left today of the wild and domestic bird life is the Bird Market and the commoner pigeons which still flock around Guinness's Brewery. There are no trees now in Pimlico to nest the crows and jackdaws since the playground was demolished, the houses with the pigeon fanciers are gone and the little white-washed cottages with their cocks and hens. The Dutch Billys in Marrowbone Lane which housed the colorful, gregarious starlings have also disappeared. The swans and waterhens glide and waggle no more upon the canal water between the Iron Bridge and Rialto because the Iron Bridge is gone and the canal extension too, drained and concreted over from James's Harbour to Suir Road Bridge.

Nanny Devesey's

Buy away, buy away, new shop open,
Ham, jam, anything you want ma'am.

Nanny's shop was in No 32 Pimlico, in a tenement house on one side of the Long Entry. It was a large red-brick house with about seven families and was slightly better kept than the other tenements, due mainly to Nanny, who wouldn't let anyone pass her shop door without asking them their business.

Nanny occupied all the rooms on the ground floor, her shop being the poky front parlour on the left. With her lived her mother, Ma Devesey and her niece, Chrissie. The right-hand front parlour was beautifully furnished and was only used to carry out important business deals with clients, pay delivery men and pow-wow in secret conclave with the Jewish money-lenders. The shop measured about nine feet by eight and four or five customers were enough to pack it. It didn't stay continuously open during the day. If business was slack Nanny would retire to the back parlour where she had her kitchen. When the shop was shut, we would shout 'Shop' down the hall and rap on the door with a coin. Nanny didn't like anyone to come down the hall and rap on her kitchen door and it was woe betide any child impatient enough to dare.

She was low-sized and very good-looking, with grey hair brushed back off her face and neatly rolled upwards round the nape of her neck. She dressed very well and always wore a fur coat going to Mass on Sundays. Her only physical defect was a limp, due to a bad foot. Anyone with a deformity got a nickname, so behind her back she was called 'Hoppy Nan'.

The shop was spotless and the counter and shelves were constantly washed down with hot water and pine disinfectant. The shelves, which were at the wall behind the counter, were lined with large glass jars of Lemon's Pure Sweets. Some of the sweets were unwrapped, showing their beautiful colours and shapes, others were in papers on which there were pictures of various fruits and crinoline ladies with umbrellas. The ones in the papers were only bought on state days and special occasions like when going on a visit to a hospital or when going out with a fella. It was traditional that the girl always bought the sweets when going on a date. The sweets were weighed in a lovely little brass scales with an oval bowl and brass weights.

Other jars contained the cheaper variety of sweets such as bull's-eyes, aniseed balls, jelly-babies, and liquorice allsorts. These were sold in pennorts and ha'ports. There were cardboard boxes with chocolate bars of every description, large bars of Cleeve's toffee, chocolate mice, marshmallows, bags of fizz with and without sticks, lucky dips and lucky balls with ha'pennies and thruppenny bits inside.

The window was decked out with big boxes of chocolates with lovely pictures, all tied up with ribbons and bows. There were lollipops, jars of marbles, spinning tops with whips, boxes of chalk, white and coloured, and gob-stoppers. Bottles of lemonade, orange and raspberry were arranged here and there and neatly piled in pyramids were the apples and oranges and bananas.

On one of the shelves behind the counter, Nanny kept the huge boxes of butter, and beside them stood the earthenware jar with water and the butter-clappers. The butter was called country butter or creamery butter, the former being cheaper. Nanny would dig out the butter with the clappers and beat it into an oblong shape, leaving lovely straight pattern lines along the length. She weighed it on a big white scales which stood on the counter beside the turnovers and loaves, rashers and sausages. On a side shelf she kept the cigarettes, matches, carbolic and Sunlight soap, Reckett's Blue and, below on the floor, bundles of sticks. Outside the counter at the door stood bags of potatoes and slatted orange boxes. Inside the counter a whole corner was given over to the paraffin oil which was held in a huge drum. The oil was pumped out with a T-shaped handle in an up-and-down movement and a tap piped it into an oil jug. There were jugs of different sizes, and when the required amount was pumped Nannie

Gob stoppers and blind mice

emptied the jug into a funnel which was stuck down into the customer's oil can, bottle or sometimes the oil-lamp itself.

When the second World War came the oranges and bananas disappeared. We particularly missed the oranges because the boxes were tied up with a straw-coloured hairy rope which we used as skipping ropes and for swinging on the lamp-posts outside Ma McCann's or up the Square. Our mothers missed them because the boxes used to be chopped up by Nannie and sold as bundles of sticks for the fires.

Nanny's wasn't simply a shop — it was an institution. Advice and sympathy were freely available, gossip, true and false, was spread, boycotts were organised and reputations were lost and gained within its portals. Nanny's was the very heart of our existence, the pulse of our street.

The shop operated on the 'tick' system. All purchases were entered into a little red-covered notebook with 'Cash' written on the cover. This was an extraordinary feat because Nanny was illiterate, but she had her own signs and symbols and what she lacked in literacy she made up for in numeracy.

The whole economy of the street revolved around the shop. Nanny and Chrissie organised the Diddly Club, the Christmas Club, the Permanent Wave Club, the Photograph Club and the Clothes Club. Wall Street never had as much monetary power.

The Jewish money-lenders were introduced to their customers through Nanny, who received a commission for her services. On the Kathleen Mavourneen system (the never-never) the tenement rooms were furnished and the walls elaborately decorated with gold-framed pictures of Pope Pius XII and large pictures of the Holy Family which were always hung over the beds. Statues of the Child of 'Prayg', as we pronounced it, statues of the Blessed Virgin and statues of the Sacred Heart, covered over with glass shades, stood on chests of drawers, mantelpieces and shelves. Some people had little altar-lamps with coloured shades lighting in front of their pictures or statues.

Besides the Jew-men there were local money-lenders who were the nearest thing to the Mafia, so people preferred to borrow from the Jew-men who were easier to shake off. Unemployment was high, wages were low and families were large, so various methods had to be devised to juggle the weekly income. Some people became so enmeshed with money-lenders, pawn offices and betting shops that they ended up totally destitute. My mother was a great one for the maxims such as 'Never a borrower or a lender be' and 'Have it yourself or be without it'. Circumstances didn't always allow her to live up to these shining principles, however, especially when large sums of money had to be laid out, such as for First Holy Communion and Confirmation outfits.

My mother's last involvement with the Jew-men was when she borrowed for my Confirmation from Mr Glick. He always called on Monday mornings for his money because he knew that Maggie Vaughan, the rent collector, also called for the rents. My mother said he was glick by name and nature, as *glic* is the Irish word for 'clever'. She found it very hard to keep up the repayments because Glick charged very high interest, so she took to walking abroad on Monday mornings. This distressed her very much because another of her shining maxims was 'Always pay the rent and keep the roof over your head.'

Mr Glick began to make a nuisance of himself. He came at all hours of the day and night, threatening the police on us. Nanny Devesey was very upset because my mother had let her down and she refused to give her any more on 'tick'. We were finally saved from the clutches of Glick when someone more *glic* discovered that he had no licence and was breaking the law. So my brother Paddy waylaid Mr Glick one night while he was on the prowl for his money, and the poor man never knew what hit him. It was now two years into the war, times were very harsh, and Paddy decided to emigrate to England. It was the first time the family had broken up, but it heralded a most dramatic change in our fortunes.

The War Years

Uncle Christy was a very quiet, cheerful man who was everybody's favourite both inside and outside the family and especially in the pubs, where he threw money around like snuff at a wake. The conditions under which he worked in the skinyard were dreadful, and for this reason allowances were always made for his excessive fondness for Guinness — he needed it to keep him going. Saturday was pay-day and half-day in Judd's, and there were times when my mother would be nearly out of her mind waiting for him to come home with the few ha'pence to buy food.

It was Stephen's job to be there waiting for Uncle Christy to remove his great big hobnailed boots and woollen stockings which were covered with blood and sheeps' wool. He was paid twopence for doing this and if ever he failed to turn up, I had to do it. When the boots and socks were removed, Christy would peel off all his soiled, smelly working clothes and my mother would immediately put them into a huge black cauldron of boiling water on the fire. A black iron kettle with more boiling water was ready waiting for the big wash down, and while Christy was doing this my mother prepared his dinner, in between poking and prodding the boiling dungarees, shirts, long drawers and vests. From the smell of the boiling clothes, the steam, the fry-up and the smoke from the fire, the water used to pour from my mother's eyes and the sweat from her brow as she tried to cope with everything at once. Uncle Paddy couldn't help because of his arthritis, granny couldn't help because she was too old, I couldn't help because I was too young and Stephen couldn't help because he was too cute and had disappeared out. 'That bloody canat is never around when he's wanted,' my mother would sigh as pots and pans slipped everyway.

Uncle Paddy would sit at the window keeping an eager eye on the proceedings like a pet dog waiting for its master to take it for a walk. As soon as Christy was washed, fed and rested, he'd give Paddy the nod and the two of them would sally forth to meet their cronies in Dwyer's pub around the Bawn or in Johnny Curran's at the corner of Engine Alley, Cremmin's at the corner of 'Breffer' Street or up in the Yanks in Marrowbone Lane, and God knows when they'd return. As soon as the door closed after them, my mother would sink down into a chair, exhausted, take out her Colman's mustard tin, take out a good pinch of snuff and with a deep sniff remark bitterly, 'There they are now, all puffed, powdered and shaved, off up to their full-bellied tricks.'

Although there were fourteen years between these two brothers and the older was dependent on the younger, they had always been pals. Their temperaments were completely different but complementary, so that when after only a few months of illness Christy died on 29 March 1939 from cancer of the throat, the light went out of Paddy's life and he would spend a lot of time in Meath Street Chapel 'doing Jack Moorhouse's Stations' as he always called my father's handiwork.

During the time he was out of work sick, Mr Judd, the owner of the skin yard, sent Christy's wages to my mother every week and when Christy died he paid all the funeral expenses. Christy's popularity was such that on the day of the funeral, all the shops and pubs in the area closed and hundreds attended the funeral to Ballyfermot graveyard. He was the last of the family to be buried there, because the graveyard was closed shortly after. It was a sad time in the street for only two days before Christy's death, his old friend and neighbour, Ma McCann, died too and she was buried in Bluebell graveyard.

His death brought us great financial hardship as he was the main bread-winner in the family. Paddy had left the Snack Sandwich Service and was now working in Tarlo's at the corner of Parliament Street opposite the *Evening Mail*. He was eighteen years of age and earning fifteen shillings a week delivering coats and suits around the city and collecting bales of material from the docks. His means of conveyance was a handcart, which had him nearly half dead. Sean was still working in the Wicklow Hotel, where he was now training to be a barman.

Although I was only eight years old I was beginning to have some idea of the happenings in the outside world. Since Uncle Christy's death and with Paddy working all day, Stephen and I fell in for the job of reading to Uncle Paddy. He didn't mind my stuttering and stumbling over words I couldn't pronounce or understand, because he was able to knock down the sense by the content. As I read the headlines, his head would shake sadly and between sucks on his dudeen he would mutter about hard times to come.

He would ask me was there any news of Frank Ryan, who was still in jail in Spain. At the mention of Franco's name he would always spit into the fire. A neighbour in the house next-door had gone off to fight in Spain with the Blueshirts and was now back living in one room with his wife, a baby and two little bonhams. The rest of the people in the house objected to the smell of the bonhams and were insisting that he get rid of them. Uncle Paddy told them to leave the little pigs alone but to get rid of the Blueshirt or they'd never be able to stick the smell in the street. I had heard him talk on occasions about King Yalla Francis but it wasn't until I began reading the papers that I came to realise that he was referring to King Alphonso.

Class of 1938 in School Street School

He was delighted to be told the good news that for the first time Irish workers could legally claim holidays with pay from their employers, for he was a great supporter of the Trade Union movement and he followed the activities of the Unemployed Workers' Association which was holding mass demonstrations in the city for work and bread. Our cousin Jem Balfe had lost his job in the Killeen Paper Mills in Bluebell and, like thousands of others, his dole was being stopped and the government was forcing the men to go to work on the bogs and to do relief work at wages below the rate. The Unemployed Workers' Association meetings and demonstrations were being broken up by the police. They carried a 'corpse' one day on a pall covered in a shroud on which was written 'To the grave with the dead, to the living, bread.' Jem came home and gave vivid descriptions of the baton charges which had taken place and how the unemployed lay down on the tram-tracks and stopped all the traffic in the city.

News from foreign parts was getting more serious and Uncle Paddy was driving us mad reading things we didn't understand or care about. He would then hold forth from his seat at the window, with the paper in his hand, informing everyone who passed by about what was happening on the international scene. He constantly referred to Hitler as the German Man and to Mr Cosgrave, whom he detested, as that Cosgrove Man. He deliberately mispronounced a name or gave a nickname to those he didn't like in order to ridicule them.

Then one day in September, in the early afternoon, didn't Johnny Tynan, Mrs Tynan and all the little barefooted Tynans, come running into Pimlico with the evening papers. Instead of yelling his usual 'Hairy-Hiock-Nuk-Noc-Na-Mayoc' Johnny was yelling 'Stop Press. Read all about it.' He had a large sheet of paper in front of him on which was written 'War Declared'. The papers were selling like hot cakes. People were buying them who never bought papers before and many of them couldn't even read what was on them. The way the grown-ups were going on it seemed quite serious. Julia Hennessy, whose husband had been wounded in the 1914–18 War, came into my mother and said, 'There ye are now, Joe got wounded for nothing. We were all told that that was going to be the war to end all wars and now, here we are again.'

That evening after tea our gang sat huddled together up the Square and we tried to figure out what it all meant. Those whose fathers had been British army soldiers were the most knowledgeable about what was going to happen, but none of us knew why there had to be a war and we all wondered where it was going to be held. Anyway we were all going to hide somewhere when it came.

As the year was coming to its end we began to form allegiances which were influenced by the talk we heard in our homes. 'Who are you up for?' Some were up for the English because they were the best and they bate the Jerries before. Others were up for the Germans because they hated the English because the English hated the Irish.

Then, just before Christmas, the IRA raided the Magazine Fort in the Phoenix Park and got away with over a million rounds of ammunition. The police swooped on the street one morning, in the early hours, and took away three of our neighbours, the brothers Dolly and Hughie Hamilton and Jack Doyle, because they were members of the IRA. Four policemen arrived at their doors in the wagon and they were taken down to the station where they were handed over to the army. From there they were taken to Arbour Hill, where, by a strange coincidence, another neighbour, Mr Cullen from the Banks of Pimlico, was put on guard over them before they were interned in the Curragh. While they were in Arbour Hill they came across another neighbour, Tommy McCann, who was also being held, but for a different reason. Tommy was an ex-British army man who had fought in the 1914 War and had come home shell-shocked. One day when he was blind drunk he went and enlisted in the Irish army and was told to come back in a week, but he forgot all about it. So, they came for him and threw him into Arbour Hill.

The room beside granny's in No 35 became vacant, and as it was bigger than the one we were living in we moved up there. It was handier too for my mother, because she no longer had to run up and down the street from one house to the other. Granny and Uncle Paddy were finding it very hard to manage on their old-age pensions. Prices had gone up and coal and paraffin oil were scarce. Both these commodities were absolutely essential to us for heat and light. They couldn't cope with the shortages of bread, butter and tea and the long queues for food and the wet turf. In the end they decided to give up their room in Pimlico and granny went to live in the Little Sisters of the Poor in Kilmainham and Uncle Paddy went to live with his sister, Maggie, in Keogh Square, Inchicore. We moved into their room, which was a large room with two windows and we gave up the back room. This arrangement didn't last for long, and after a few months they were pining for Pimlico. Then Julia Mac died in No 33 and they both returned and rented her room. The position was now reversed — we were in their room and they were in the house which we had left.

The government had introduced a fuel scheme for those on the windows', old-age and blind pensions and the unemployed. This entitled the households in each of these categories to eight stone of turf per week. Dockets were issued at post offices and labour exchanges and cost sixpence to my mother and granny. The turf had to be collected at turf depots and ours was in Bridgefoot Street. At first we used pay a man a shilling to deliver it on a handcart which he and others likewise engaged hired out from a place in Granby Lane for one shilling a day. Every Friday morning my mother would go down and join the queue outside the fuel depot and it was a heart-breaking sight to see the very old and the poorly clad shivering and unprotected from the elements. We had to provide our own sacks or bags and the fellas weighing the turf showered heaps of abuse at the people and gave them short weight. Sometimes the turf was so wet that the people said it should have been piped.

The fellas with the handcarts would pile up several deliveries and take the dockets which had the peoples' addresses and then set off. As soon as they got out of sight they would transfer some of the turf into empty sacks and leave the people short. There were times when they didn't deliver at all and people were left without any firing, or they would rob good sacks and substitute old and torn ones in their place.

Women and children pushing home the turf

Many of the people in the street, particularly the old, couldn't cope with these fly-by-nights or the wet turf which wouldn't light or with having to stand out in the cold, the rain and the snow, so they would sell their turf docket for a shilling to one of the neighbours. Julia Hennessy gave my mother a big, old broken-down pram and she would have to make two journeys up Bridgefoot Street hill, pushing the eight stone of turf each time. It nearly killed her, although at times she would get help from a passer-by at the last steep bit of the hill. In the end she had to wait until I came home from school when I would go on ahead and take my place in the queue at the depot with one of my pals. When the sacks were filled up with the sodden turf my pal Kathleen Fortune would stand guard over two sacks while my mother and I would push the other two up the hill. Once at the top we would remove the two sacks outside Thomas Street Post Office and my mother would stand guard over them while I accelerated down the hill to Kathleen and we would then repeat the uphill journey with the rest of the turf. At the top of the hill we would nearly break our backs trying to fit the hundredweight of turf onto the pram before setting off down Thomas Court. My mother was mortified with all of this, while Kathleen and I thought it great gas and we'd fall around the road laughing whenever the turf collapsed all over the road or one of the wheels came off the pram.

At home my mother would bank the turf up on the hobs and round the back of the fire hoping that the heat from the fire would help to dry out the turf. All the people in the tenements had to do this, and on occasions it proved a very dangerous practice because it would catch light, set the chimneys on fire and buckets of water would have to be thrown on the fire, leaving the people worse off than before. The amount of worry, trouble and hardship that so-called free fuel caused had to be seen to be believed.

Stephen was just fourteen years of age and was in the seventh class in Francis Street Christian Brothers and was learning nothing more than he had learned in sixth class, so when Miss Rigney, the tobacconist at the corner of Meath Street and Gray Street, said she was looking for a messenger boy to deliver the newspapers and the comics for five shillings a week, my mother asked her to take on Stephen. During his free hours from Rigney's he would go with his pals gathering cinders in the tip-head and sell them round the houses, or he would chop up tree blocks and sell bundles of sticks. There was quite a demand for these, especially from those who had only the fire to cook on. Gas was rationed, which meant that the neighbours in the Artisans' Dwellings were doing more cooking on their fires also.

On 3 January 1943 I was woken up by an enormous bang, which at first I thought was thunder. My mother and I were sleeping head to tail in a wooden chair-bed, and I remember holding onto her feet in terror. Sean was sitting bolt upright in the bed by the wall and he calmly said, 'We are being bombed — listen.' Sure enough, we could hear the drone of a plane, then a high-pitched whistle getting nearer and then another almighty explosion. We were terrified because it all sounded so near. We assumed that it was the Germans, thinking that the English couldn't possibly make such a geographical mistake. It didn't last very long, and then we heard the low drone of a plane receding. We looked out the window and there was great commotion in the street with the neighbours across the road standing on the footpath looking up at the search-lights, criss-crossing each other as they swept across the sky. Next morning we learned from our neighbours who had radios that the South Circular Road had been bombed and that the Synagogue had been badly damaged. Rumours ran riot and we were now more convinced than ever that it had been a German plane and that the Jews had been the target.

Paddy was getting tired trotting between the shafts of Tarlo's handcart and as the price of everything had gone up and his wages hadn't, he put in for an increase. Mr Tarlo couldn't believe his ears and refused Paddy's request point blank. So Paddy joined the ranks of the unemployed. The government had introduced a scheme for the unemployed in an attempt to encourage them to grow their own vegetables. Plots of land measuring an eighth of an acre were rented out for 1/- per week so Paddy and a few of the lads around decided to put their shoulders to the plough. They planted cabbages, carrots, scallions and potatoes and we were all looking forward to a bumper harvest.

However, Paddy got restless before the crop was ready. Many of the unemployed were taking the boat to England where plenty of work and high wages attracted them like magnets, but Paddy had a problem — he wasn't old enough. Permits to emigrate were only given to those who had reached the age of twenty-one years, but he overcame this by using Sean's birth certificate. My mother didn't want him to go, but she had to accept his departure like all the other women in the street whose sons, daughters and husbands also left, some of them never to return, while others were back within the week.

Johnny Ennis from Thomas Court, who had worked on the plots with Paddy, came up one day to my mother to tell her that the vegetables were now ready for digging and that she should get someone to take them up. She got two someones, me and Stephen. The plots were up in Ballyfermot, a place we knew very well, because all our relations on my mother's side were buried up there. Johnny Ennis gave us the number of Paddy's plot, and so one sunny Saturday morning we set sail with the turf pram and a small child's spade which we used for taking up the ashes. We had the two turf sacks as well to hold the booty.

It's a fine step from Pimlico to Ballyfermot and we were exhausted by the time we got there even though we gave each other jaunts in the pram. We found the plots and Paddy's number and then we cast about for the vegetables. The cabbages were easy enough to find and the scallions and by a stroke of good detective work Stephen found the carrots, but the potatoes were nowhere to be seen. In the distance there were a couple of men working at their plots and they paid no attention to us.

We yanked all the cabbages out of the ground, likewise the scallions and carrots. Stephen cut the stalks off the cabbages and we pulled the green ferns off the carrots. Even so, we found it hard to fit them all into the sacks. then quite by accident Stephen came across a few potatoes lying in a ridge and he pulled at this big plant, and lo and behold, several lovely potatoes appeared at the roots. We then set to work with a will, racing each other to see who could pull the most. Before long there were hundreds of potatoes strewn around, and as we had been working for hours and our backs were broken we decided to call it a day. What we couldn't fit into the sacks we shoved down into the empty spaces in the pram and we set off for home, well pleased with the day's work. The masey was going to be delighted with all this grub.

With great difficulty we got out onto the road and headed east. Not a soul was in sight and the countryside looked lovely. To shorten the road we struck up a few patriotic marching songs of which Stephen had hundreds which he had learned at the Christian Brothers. Suddenly, from out of a side-road, a figure in black appeared on the scene, riding a big upstairs model. When it saw us it turned in our direction and at about twenty yards from us it dismounted and walked slowly by the side of the bicycle towards us.

My heart started to race because I was terrified of policemen and Stephen hated them. This one was wearing a flat hat which wasn't like the city policeman's hat, and around his shoulders he wore a short cape. I was hoping he would pass us by, but Stephen, who knew better, muttered under his breath, 'Keep your mouth shut, d'ye hear, and stop looking so bloody guilty.'

The policeman stopped dead in front of us. 'What have you got there?'

'Vegetables,' said Stephen.

'I can see that. And where did you get them? You stole them from the plots above, I suppose. Is that right?'

'Oh, no sir,' I put in quickly. 'We dug them out of our brother's plot. He grew them for us. We didn't steal them, honest.' The tears began to run down my cheeks as Stephen began to explain that Paddy was sick and couldn't come and we needed the vegetables for the dinner.

'It would take you a year to eat all that you have there. Open up those sacks and throw that stuff out onto the road. Be quick about it. I'll soon find out what this is all about.'

As he was saying this his hand went up to his breast pocket and he opened the button and took out a pencil and notebook. When I saw this I became hysterical and the prediction that Sr Selsus had made in school, that I would one day end up in jail and be hanged, seemed to be coming true. Stephen didn't know what to do. He was torn between righteous indignation at the bobby's high-handedness and my uncontrollable shaking and crying. We nearly killed ourselves trying to take the sacks off the pram and then we emptied them all over the road, while he took our names and address, Paddy's name and plot number.

'Right, I'll investigate immediately. Clear up and clear off. If I find out that you've been telling me lies, I'll have you both brought before the magistrate. Is that understood?' He put his foot on the pedal and gave himself a push with his other foot and then he swung himself into the saddle and cycled slowly away.

We began to pick up the vegetables and when we thought that he was gone far enough away we looked up the road after him. He was well out of earshot when Stephen began to call him all the names going, then he turned on me and called me all the yalla-necked, white-livered bitches going, and blamed it all on me with my guilty red face and my whinging and whining and my 'sir' this and my 'sir' that. That was the last straw and I refused to help to pick up the vegetables until Stephen pointed out that if I didn't help, the flat-footed effer would be back down the road and then I'd be sorry.

It was teatime before we reached Pimlico and my mother was nearly out of her mind with worry, which disappeared when she saw the spoils. Josie, who lived in the parlour, came out when she heard us struggling with the sacks up the stairs. We spilled the contents out on the floor and began sorting them out. Josie was bawling all over the place in her usual raucous fashion, falling around the room as our confrontation with the policeman was told. Nan upstairs heard the commotion and came down to investigate and she had to be told and the more it was told the more Josie roared.

Kate next-door came in from the shops and her eyes nearly popped out when she saw the scene. Before long the room was packed with neighbours and they all took their share of the vegetables. Coarse aprons, pots, basins and buckets were used to take them away. For a week we were eating cabbage and potatoes every day and the smell of boiled cabbage never left the house for a month.

Johnny Ennis came looking for Stephen a few days later saying that he was going to break every bone in his body for destroying and robbing, not only his plot but also the plots of other men and when Stephen heard this he went on 'gur' for a week.

The Swingin' Boats was closed for a time while air-raid shelters were being dug and another shelter was built down on the Banks. The ones in the playground were locked and the one on the Banks became a great place for hiding and courting until, in time, it began to be used as a dump. The ARP men would come around now and again to give us directions on what to do in case of an air attack and then one day everyone was issued with a card to go up to Guinness's Dining Rooms to be fitted for gas masks. This was great fun for us and we came away with a cardboard box and a quare-looking yoke each which we regarded as a fantastic toy. Luckily, we never had any occasion to use them, for with playing with them up and down the street, they were in bits before long.

Since gas rationing had been introduced, the glimmerman was a regular visitor in the street although it didn't affect us since we hadn't got the gas. The glimmerman was an official who came around to check that people were not cooking on the 'glimmer', a small stream of gas that leaked into people's cookers even when the supply was rationed and cut off. Three of the tenement houses had gas, and whenever we saw the glimmerman arrive in the street we would run up the houses as well as knocking on the Artisans' Dwellings doors to warn them of imminent danger, because very heavy fines were imposed on those caught, and some had the gas cut off altogether. A song we used sing went:

Strike a match and turn the glimmer on,
Strike a match and turn the glimmer on,
When you hear the kids all shout
Run like the divil and turn the glimmer out,
When you hear the kids all cry, 'the glimmerman is gone'
Then one, two, three, all together with me,
Strike a match and turn the glimmer on.

Everything had become very scarce, money, food, clothes and tobacco. The only thing that seemed to be thriving was the black market. There was usually someone able to pooch around and find a shop that had just got in paraffin oil, tea or butter and the word would spread like wildfire. Nanny and Mary Roach, two elderly sisters who had a shop at the corner of the Green Yard on the Banks, were great for getting in the drop of paraffin at odd times. They also kept the locals supplied with cigarettes called Tento, Drumhead and Stars. They would sell the cigarettes singly and they also sold stale cigarettes and matches. The shops would hide the cigarettes under the counter and oul' Johnny Egan, who had a shop at the edge of the Bawn, rolled cigarettes in a little machine and sold them for a penny each. The people were robbed with all this carry-on, particularly when it came to tea. My mother was told about a pub in North King Street, nearly opposite Green Street, that was selling tea at two and six an ounce, at a time when the proper price was three and four a pound. It sold snuff as well, in a little bag shaped like a triangle, which suited her down to the ground, as she was fond of a pinch, so she would belt over the Liffey and take her place in the blackmarket queue. As luck would have it wasn't the owner of the pub caught and charged, not for selling the blackmarket tea, but because someone reported that the tea was mixed with sawdust to bring up the weight.

Clothes rationing didn't affect us all that much since we bought ours second-hand. Granny and Uncle Paddy bought no clothes at all, so we had their coupons, and Sean, who had to dress properly for the Wicklow Hotel, was able to use them.

Paddy was now working in England and was writing home regularly. He seemed to be changing his address every few months as well as his jobs. Sean hadn't been too content since Paddy's departure as they had always knocked around together and Sean missed the company. So one day he announced that he was going to pack up his job in the hotel and join Paddy in England. This my mother definitely didn't agree with, because his job in the hotel had been a good one and there was no need for him to go away. We all went with him down to Westland Row Station and on the way down Pearse Street we were accompanied by crowds of others going in the same direction. The station was packed, but only those travelling were allowed on the platform. People were crying and hugging each other and everyone was promising to write to everyone else. Some were carrying large suitcases, others small school cases, but many were clutching brown paper parcels. My mother was crying but Sean seemed anxious to go so we bade him farewell. The war was over before we saw him again.

There were great changes taking place in the street. Many of our old neighbours died, some in their own rooms, others in the Union in James's Street. Granny and Uncle Paddy were about the last of their generation, and in 1943 Uncle Paddy, who was now totally crippled with sciatica and was hardly able to breathe with bronchitis had to go into the Union as well, where he died just before his seventy-seventh birthday. The following year granny had to go to the Union too, where she died at the age of eighty-three. My mother had looked after them until she could no longer lift them or attend to their needs. They were hoping that they would die at home and expressed this wish many times, because they dreaded the thoughts of going into the Union. I will never forget how awful a place it was as every Thursday and Sunday we lined up outside the big gate in James's Street waiting for it to open, while inside in the grounds the poor paupers, in their worsted grey suits and other institutional garb, wandered aimlessly or sat on seats gazing blankly into space.

The young were dying too. TB or, as we called it, galloping consumption, was wiping out whole families. In one large family who lived opposite to us, six of the children died. Each :ime a case was diagnosed in the house, the van from the Corporation disinfectant yard in Marrowbone Lane would come down and take away all the bed-linen and clothes and take them up to be fumigated. The house was also fumigated. This was very humiliating for the families because it advertised to all the world that there was TB in the house and people were very sensitive about it. They thought of it as a shameful disease and they didn't want to admit to having it. A number of my school pals died and I lived in fear and dread of becoming infected.

The Corporation was offering houses to some of the large families in the tenements and a few of them left and went off to live in North Crumlin, but the high rents and the lack of amenities had them back in a couple of months looking for rooms again. This was the cause of many a row, because when some tenants left a room to go to a Corporation house they'd sell the key for between five and seven pounds depending on the size of the room and where it was situated in the house. The rent collector, Maggie Vaughan, wouldn't be aware of this transaction and to keep it secret, a child would be sent up to Maggie in Braithwaite Street with the rent from Mrs So-and-so. The returned tenant, who had never handed up the rent book, still considered herself to be the legal tenant of the room and would create desolation trying to evict the newcomer. It was very difficult for a newly wed couple to get a room in the street or a family with small children and so they were only too willing to pay the key-money and risk being evicted.

The winds of change were blowing and homes were being broken up either through emigration or the deaths of the very old and the young. Our family was now reduced to my mother and myself, Stephen having gone to the Construction Corps. Sean and Paddy had been sending money every week from England and we were no longer in dire straits, in fact we were never as well off. When I needed clothes now my mother lost the head and had them made to measure in McDonald's of Thomas Street. When Sean had worked in the Wicklow Hotel he had been regularly supplied with complimentary theatre tickets and over the years my mother and I had seen many shows. She was as proud as a queen now at being able to go to the box-office and book. Even the food we ate was different for there was no more cow-heel, tripe, pigs' cheeks or feet, although the manner of cooking remained the same — on the open fire.

35 Pimlico,
Dublin.
26th August 1945

Dear Sir / Madam,

In reply to your advertisement in to-day's Evening Mail, seeking a learner in your esteemed blouse factory, I wish to offer myself as a candidate for the position.

I am 14 years of age and attended the Holy Faith National School, the Coombe, where I reached 6th Standard and obtained the Primary Certificate.

If you favour me with the position I will do my utmost to give every satisfaction.

Awaiting the favour of your reply.

Yours sincerely,
Máirín Moorhouse.

Our Childhood

Our childhood, such as it was, didn't last very long and we then entered into a period of naive adulthood — teenagers hadn't yet been invented. Although school was compulsory up to the age of fourteen years, many of my school friends left in their thirteenth years and one or two of them became mothers without the rest of us knowing they were even pregnant.

As the end of our schooling approached, we were psychologically prepared, both at home and at school, for the world of work, the labour market. Before the happy hour of release arrived, our parents scanned the 'Situations Vacant' in the *Evening Mail,* exclaiming sadly at the grand little situations at seven and six and ten shillings a week, then going a-begging that couldn't be applied for just yet. Sr Pascal showed us how to sell ourselves to the employers — who were all very decent people and very kind to even bother offering us work — by replying to advertisements correctly. Our passport to a good, steady job was the Primary Certificate and without this the quality of our lives would not improve. This was the letter we were taught to write:

Address

Date

Dear Sir/Madam,

In reply to your advertisement in today's *Evening Mail* (or whatever) seeking a learner in your esteemed blouse factory, I wish to offer myself as a candidate for the position. I am fourteen years of age and attended the Holy Faith National School, the Coombe, where I reached the sixth standard and obtained the Primary Certificate.

If you favour me with the position I will do my utmost to give every satisfaction. Awaiting the favour of your reply.

Yours sincerely,
Full name.

When the time came for me to leave school, I was most reluctant to go out into the unknown. I immediately set about the task of getting a job and I must have written the words of the correct way to reply to an advertisement about a million times and eventually came to the conclusion that the employers couldn't read because I never once got a reply. Years later, when I had a bit more savvy, I realised that the employers and the entire office staffs of the firms I wrote to must have been twisted with laughter at the servile tone of the letter, especially the back-alley factories whose standing was anything but 'esteemed.'

Most of the girls in the street worked in various kinds of sewing factories, Polikoffs Tailoring having the most prestige and highest wages. Others worked in the Mount Brown Laundry, Donnolly's Bacon Factory in Cork Street and Jacob's Biscuit Factory. One or two worked as cleaners, but this was work which was mainly done by married women who could find no other employment or those who were considered unfit for other employment. Guinness's cleaners were different — they got their jobs by virtue of the fact that they were widows or relations of Guinness's workers.

Married women were barred from working in many sewing factories and employers sacked their women workers on marriage so that women were forced to become very secretive about their nuptials. The Hennessys and the McCanns from Pimlico were past masters at the art of concealing, not only their marriages but also the births of their children which used cause great amusement up to the point when they'd be found out and sacked. Under these circumstances a few married women in the street had to go into the home-dressmaking market, making clothes for the neighbours or for small local shops or as out-workers for employers who paid them almost in buttons.

The boys who left school at this time fared no better than the girls. They began their working lives as messenger boys, carrying enormous heavy awkward loads in huge baskets on the fronts of their bicycles. Some of them couldn't reach the pedals without standing up and it was not an unfamiliar sight to see one sprawled on the roadway, with goods and broken bottles strewn in every direction. That's why granny prayed so earnestly for Sean. A grade higher than messenger boy was van-boy on milkvans, breadvans, laundry-vans or a carter's help on a dray or best of all a Guinness's messenger with a nice little uniform and cap.

The working day in Pimlico began at the unearthly hour of half past five in the morning when the people of the Artisans' Dwellings who worked in Guinness's came to life and set out for the early shift. The heavy tread of the men's boots and the low murmur of their voices as they greeted each other on the way to the brewery roused those of us who lived in the front rooms, and for my mother this was the signal to rise and shine. Her first job was to clear out the ashes and light the fire, go down the stairs and out the yard for the water and then put the kettle on. Her next job was to wake up Billser Byrne who lived in the room next door to ours.

Billser was a casual labourer up on the canal in James's Harbour, where he loaded and unloaded grain and turf. He needed to be up with the birds but even so he very often didn't get

Johnson collection/RTE

Catching pinkeens in the canal opposite Forbe's Lane, 1952

the worms. Many, many times Billser would return home disappointed to his mother Kate, who as well as being a very old friend of the family was also a relation by marriage to my mother, her daughter having married my mother's Uncle Stephen. At the crack of dawn, in all weather, Billser took his stand at the harbour, hoping to be picked for a day's work. His problem was that he wasn't a buttonman, meaning he wasn't in the union, and all the buttonmen were picked first from among the hopeful labourers. Union men were often left standing too, when work was slack, but Billser rarely got a full week's work. My mother hadn't an ounce of sympathy for him and she'd keep at him to join the union, but she did feel sorry for Kate who whined and moaned that Billser was too 'mane' to join his hands never mind the union.

The next morning call was the postman. We had a regular who had been delivering the post for years and he always arrived between half-past seven and eight o'clock. As soon as he came into the hall he let a roar and everyone came out to see who the letter was for. If it happened to be a postcard everyone read it before the owner could take possession. The funniest situations arose when several families of the same name resided in the one house. This was the case in No 55, where four families of Cullens lived and only one of these wasn't related to the other three. The confusion was compounded when Christian names or initials were the same also. Whenever they got a letter, the four families would converge in the hall around the postman and the puzzle as to who the letter was for could only be solved at times by getting the postman to open up the envelope to see who it was from.

To cope with the volume of post coming from emigrants during and after the war, we had three deliveries a day — early morning, mid-morning and afternoon. My mother also had a regular weekly visit from the telegram boy who brought the money from the brothers in England. She was always afraid of this going astray so from ten o'clock every Saturday morning I would have to keep my eye to business for the motor-bike on which the telegram boy usually travelled. This look-out was occasioned after one telegram boy, who couldn't be bothered to call out the name and wait, shoved the telegram under Josie Moody's door, whereupon it was eagerly devoured by Josie's dog.

For the slackers who were still in bed after half-past seven, the altarboys in St Catherine's in Meath Street took great pleasure in ringing them up at ten minutes to eight and they never drew rein until eight o'clock. Then Jacob's hooter would give a short almighty blast and if you weren't in the gate of the factory when that went off you had to wait an hour before you could get in.

The people in the Liberties depended on these regular morning sounds to tell them the time of day and if for any reason one of them failed to function it was the subject of much comment. Their regularity brought an element of security to life, a feeling that what should be happening was happening. The sounds, the smells, the factories, the people, were as strands of thread weaving in and out, blending here and there, creating the daily pattern of life in the Liberties.

As I got older I began to notice that things in the street were not quite as they had been. In the early forties an outbreak of foot-and-mouth disease brought ruin to some of our local dairy and cattle owners. Mr Cassidy, who had his cows up at the top of the Green Yard, lost all his herd, and Mick Russell in Marrowbone Lane was also badly hit. Outbreaks of swine fever in the piggeries brought hardship also to the families whose livelihood for generations had centred around these animals. Mr Cassidy ended up selling turf and blocks and some of the piggeries were closed down. Only the owners mourned their passing.

My first year after leaving school was taken up mostly by slogging it around the city, knocking on little office windows, ringing bells, climbing endless stairs in large tenement houses where back-street factories were located, offering my services, with my school reference and my baptismal lines becoming more dog-eared with time. I was only one of thousands doing the same and the people in the offices were sick to death of the constant question, 'Any vacancies please?' Some of them would nearly take the nose off us with the shutter on the office window and they were all but short of setting ferocious unmuzzled animals on our heels.

It was then that I also noticed that there weren't so many children knocking around the street, either. Emigration and departures to new housing estates had reduced the young population and the Swingin' Boats was often locked and chained during the day. Some of the swings were missing and the fly-pole was gone and the skittle-alley had long since disappeared. Looking through the railings at the empty playground brought home to me more than anything else that the noisy, carefree, happy days were over. Poor 'oul' McGowan, the cock of the town' had found peace at last. Many of the old neighbours had died and their rooms were being let to strangers from other areas and slowly but surely the character of the street was changing.

Across the road, the Protestant population was decreasing also. My older brothers' friends, Freddie Hill and Seamus King and their families had moved off to God knows where to be followed some years later by Lottie Wilson and her parents. One of the Langs became a Catholic and married a Catholic and the Colemans from No 59 won the sweep and moved around to Hanbury Lane. At the end of 1952, the Quakers left their Meeting House in Meath Place (Cole Alley) where they had been since 1665 and they transferred to their premises in Eustace Street. St. Catherine's Church in Thomas Street and St Nicholas Without and St Luke were losing their parishioners and it was becoming increasingly difficult to maintain the churches. The Catholic churches were also showing signs of loss as the life-blood of the Liberties was being insidiously drained away.

One day a terrible tragedy occurred which shocked us all. Mr Maher, an elderly neighbour, who lived with Mrs Maher and their Irish terrier, Paddy, in No 45, cut his throat with a razor. He never spoke much to anyone around and they were regarded as a quiet, inoffensive old couple. When the weather was fine and warm, Mr Maher and Paddy, the dog, would sit outside their house watching the world go by. When eventually the house became vacant everybody in the street was saying that nobody would live in it, but they were wrong because it wasn't long empty. Attitudes were changing too.

The year I left school the war ended and before the bells of Christchurch Cathedral had rung the old year out I got a job in Gordon and Thompson's shirt factory in Francis Street for nine and elevenpence a week, standing all day from 9 a.m. to 6 p.m., clipping threads from the finished articles. My mother gave me a shilling a week pocket money until at the end of two months I was put onto a felling machine, went onto piece-work, earned between twenty-five and thirty shillings a week and gave my mother a pound. The forewoman was an ancient battle-axe from Derry, who wouldn't allow us to open the one and only window, which was up in the roof and for two and a half years all the workers were choked with the starch and dust which flew out of the shirts, dungarees and pyjamas. My friend Marie got TB and so also did some of the older workers but Miss McGinley still wouldn't open the window. In the end I was sacked because a little bird told her I was trying to start a union. Maybe it was just as well, for I'm convinced that there must be a shirtmaker's equivalent of coal-miner's pneumoconiosis. Against my mother's wishes, I became a Jacob's 'rossie' and nearly killed myself throwing 'mix' down from the marshmallow loft through a hole in the ceiling on to the Coconut Creams, Mikado and Kimberly biscuits. At this point I became the sole support in the home, the three brothers having got married, and our standard of living plummeted drastically.

The tenement houses were looking more dilapidated than ever. For years no repairs had been carried out and when a good shower of rain came down it poured through the holes in the roof. Nan Murray had to catch the streams of water in buckets and basins. It ran down the walls into our room below and stained the ceiling and the wallpaper bulged out and fell off. Our outer wall at the fountain was crumbling away worse than ever, particularly when heavy lorries and vans came round the corner. The lovely fountain and the two small gardens which had once graced the side wall on the site of the court-house were smashed and barren due to lack of care and attention.

Now and again, well-heeled, articulate men from the Corporation would come round to visit us, carrying plans and papers, to ask us questions, write down answers and go away. Rumours ran riot after each visit — the houses were going to be pulled down, a new road was going to be made, we were all going to be sent out to North Crumlin, Drimnagh, Kimmage or maybe, God forbid, Cabra. It sounded like we were going to be sent to outer Siberia. The elderly people got very worried because it was rumoured that they weren't going to be housed — they'd have to look out for rooms or take sub-standard accommodation in other areas. People began to get very unsettled especially when Maggie Vaughan told us that she would no longer be coming around for the rents because the houses had been sold to a new landlord.

No 34 developed a big crack down the front and huge wooden beams were hammered into the wall to shore it up. Many of the old tenants such as Duckser Healy, his family and pigeons, the Barrys, the Foys, Brigie Egan, and Tommy Waters and his Aunt Esther were all gone. It had been customary on Thursday nights for those who couldn't read or write to come to my mother to have their pension books signed, beside which they marked their X. They were demented with worry at the uncertainty of the future. 'What are we going to do, Maggie, if we are all scattered to the four winds? Who will we get to sign the oul' pension books and sign our forms and the like? 'Clare to God things is comin' to a sorry pass. Where is it all goin' to end?'

It was all going to end in demolition, not only of the houses but also of the old community way of life. The Corporation made a compulsory purchase order entitled the Marrowbone

Gordon & Thompson's Shirt Factory

Lane and Pimlico Compulsory Purchase Order, 1954, whereby it was proposed to demolish seventy-six houses and thirty-one shops and about 500 people in the area would have to be rehoused.

At a local government inquiry into the proposed compulsory purchase order it was stated that the houses were insanitary and unfit for human habitation. Mr D. Walsh, solicitor for Dublin Corporation, said that most of the houses dated back to the eighteenth century and the only remedy was to knock them down. Mr J. A. Culleton, of the City Architects Department, described them as 'higgledy-piggledy' developments of old Huguenot and Georgian houses and Mr P. Cohen, Chief Health Inspector, said that this was possibly one of the oldest and most obsolete parts of the city! The City Medical Officer voiced the opinion that the area had outlived its economic usefulness. It was proposed to build 250 flats, of which sixteen on the ground floor would be for old people and the cost might be £500,000.

My mother was now living alone, as I had got married. Gradually the rooms became vacant as the Corporation offered those with two or more in the family flats in Donore Avenue, Dolphin House, Fatima Mansions and houses in Ballyfermot, Captains Lane and other estates. Handcarts, horses and drays and asses and carts were used to remove their furniture and my mother would sit at the window, sadly watching her friends and neighbours depart. In the end she was the only one left in the house and she'd constantly enquire at the Housing Department in Cork Hill if there was any suitable place for her to go to at a rent which she could pay. She made it clear that she didn't want to leave the Liberties but she didn't want to go to another tenement from where she might have to move again. There was nothing for her so she sat tight hoping that in the end she would be properly accommodated. After all, she reasoned, hadn't her family lived in the street for generations, and she was entitled to get a proper place. A fighter all her life, she was now taking on the Corporation, but she was alone and she was old and she was incapable of understanding the mindless bureaucrats who demolish old communities in order to widen roads.

She realised what she was up against when early one morning she arose as usual, took the water jug and went to go down stairs to the yard for water. She had descended only a few steps when she disappeared into space and landed heavily down below. During the night someone had removed the remaining wooden stairs and as her hearing wasn't good she hadn't heard a thing. She lay there unable to get up until my arrival at midday when I found her very badly bruised and very, very shaken. We never found out who took the stairs but she was convinced that the Corporation had something to do with it because they wanted her out as she was holding up the demolition. We put forward the theory that it might have been someone who simply wanted the wood to sell for firewood, but she said that the Corporation was so fed-up with her constant badgering that they'd do anything to get rid of her.

Whatever the reason, one thing was for sure, she couldn't stay in Pimlico any longer. It took a few days to get her a room in St Ultan's Flats in Charlemont Street, and one day in 1957 Stephen hired a handcart from Granby Lane and we piled my mother's home on top. With Stephen between the shafts we set sail. My mother, Paddy and I took up the rear and as we gave Stephen the initial push to set the cart in motion, I couldn't help thinking how sad an occasion this was for my mother. She had already said her farewells to the old neighbours whose families had been in the Artisans' Dwellings since they were built, so she walked down the street behind her bits and pieces, as she called them, and never as much as looked back .once, not even when we rounded the corner of the Swingin' Boats into Meath Place. She showed no sign of emotion because she was never a one for revealing her inner feelings, but I knew that inside she was crying.

My mother and her neighbours weren't sorry to see the end of the tenements but they couldn't understand why, with so many derelict sites around, new accommodation hadn't been built and the old community preserved by phasing the redevelopment. This would have prevented the displacement of hundreds of people whose roots for many generations were firmly embedded in the Liberties soil. Unfortunately for the inhabitants of Pimlico who were ousted from their native sod, the Liberties Association wasn't in existence at the time, so there was nothing around which to form a protest. The Association wasn't formed until ten years on and after ten years' more decay and demolition and hundreds more displacements.

Every day for three years, my mother walked from Charlemont Street to Thomas Street and Meath Street to do her shopping and to meet and talk to her old cronies, many of them doing the same as herself, travelling in from 'foreign' parts. None of them were happy in exile and they were always on the look-out for rooms anywhere in the area, which would bring them back to the old way of living close to each other. Finally, my granny's sister, Maggie, managed to get my mother a room near her in Allingham Buildings, off Marrowbone Lane. The houses in Pimlico by this time had been demolished and so also was the Bawn and part of Earl Street. It made the street look very different being able to look up Thomas Court from the end of Marrowbone Lane. In 1964 flats were constructed on part of the site, but to this day the spot whereon stood the ancient Courthouse, the lovely fountain and our house is vacant, an invisible monument to 'progress'.

> The house I was reared in is but a stone on a stone
> And all round the garden weeds they have grown,
> And all the fond neighbours that ever I knew
> Like the red rose they have faded in the May morning dew.

THE BANKS OF PIMLICO

One evening here not long ago through Thomas Street I strayed
And fell into conversation with a charming fair young maid
Who said she was a milliner and her name was Katy Roe
And her father kept a twang shop on the Banks of Pimlico.

We wandered on to Echlin Street and down through sweet Belview
And for a dram we both stepped into the Widda Donahoe
Whilst there Katy said to me there's an Entry here below
Which leads from Earl Street to where I live on the Banks of Pimlico.

We both went down this Entry and I nearly died with fright
When at a hall Kate let a bawl, 'Mary Ann throw down a light'
A candle came down in a flash and upstairs we did go
And Kate persuaded me to rest a while in Pimlico.

The neighbours were assembled seated round a roarin' fire
There were fiddlers and tin-whistlers and the piper Matty Maguire
The porter flowed as freely as the Poddle down below
And the divil a wan was sober that night in Pimlico.

Soon after my arrival I was called on for a song
So I obliged the company with 'The Hackler from Grouse Hall'
Then Katie's da, the Twangman sang of times long long ago
When skills and crafts were in demand round the Banks of Pimlico.

I was feeling rather drowsey after several balls of malt
When 'Rise-a-Row' from Tripoli brought the hooley to a halt
He said I'd stolen Kate, his mot, and said I had better go
Or he'd take my sacred life upon the Banks of Pimlico.

Now to conclude my story and to leave things all aside
I'm courtin' Kate the milliner in the hopes she'll be my bride
If she agrees to marry me then we'll settle down, I know
In a room above the twang shop on the Banks of Pimlico.

As sung by the author's mother.

The Banks of Pimlico.

One eve-ning here not long a-go through Tho-mas Street I strayed and fell in-to con-ver-sat-ion with a charm-ing fair young maid who said she was a mill-in-er and her name was Ka-tie Roe, and her Fa-ther kept a Twang shop on the Banks of Pim-li-co.

The house I was reared in is but a stone on a stone, and all 'round the gar-den the weeds they have grown, and all the fond neigh-bours that e—ver I knew, like the red rose they have fa-ded in the May mor-ning dew

BIBLIOGRAPHY

Rev Elliott, *Abbey and Courthouse of St Thomas*, Dublin 1892.

John Gilbert, *Calendar of Ancient Record of Dublin*, Dublin 1864.

Warburton, Whitelaw and Walshe, *A History of the City of Dublin*, London 1818.

Thom's Directory.

G. N. Wright, *A Historical Guide of the City of Dublin*, Reprint 2nd edition, Dublin 1980. First published London 1825.

Mc Cready, *Dublin Street Names*, Dublin 1892.

D. A. Chart, *The Story of Dublin*, London 1932.

Dublin Corporation Minutes and Reports 1870-1929.

The Irish Builder 1893-1898.

Viator, *Letter to the Right Hon Robert Peel*, Dublin 1816.

Newspaper Cuttings, D.A.D. Properties, Dublin.

Autobiography of Sir Charles Cameron, Dublin 1920.

H.M. Government, *Report on Housing Conditions of the Working Classes*, London and Dublin 1914.

Dr T. W. Grimshaw, *Housing Accommodation of the Artisan*, Dublin 1885.

Dr T. W. Grimshaw, *Remarks on Prevalence and Distribution of Fever in Dublin*, Dublin 1872.

Sir Charles Cameron, *How the Poor Live*, Dublin 1908.

Sir Charles Cameron, *A Brief History of Municipal Public Health*, Dublin 1914.

12th Earl of Meath, *Memories of the Nineteenth Century*, New York 1923.

Countess of Meath's Dairies, London 1900.

Most Rev Fr N. Donnelly, *History of Dublin Parishes*, Dublin (n.d.).

Helen Clayton, *To School Without Shoes*, A Brief History of the Sunday School Society for Ireland 1809-1979, Dublin (n.d.).

Census 1901-1911.

John Devoy, *Recollections*, Shannon 1969. First edition New York 1929.

Katherine O'Shea, *Charles Stewart Parnell*, Vol. II, London 1914.

Reports of the Philanthropic Reform Association 1986-1901.

Iveagh Trust Golden Jubilee Report 1909-1959.

James Collins, *Life in Old Dublin*, Dublin 1913.

Local Government & Public Health Reports, Dublin 1927-1931, 1935-1937, 1940-1943.

Stowers Johnson, *Before and After Puck Fair*, London (n.d.).

Catherine Callery, Queen's Institute of Jubilee Nurses, Dublin 1930.

Madame de Bovet, *A Three Month Tour of Ireland*, London 1891.

Sarah Davies, *St Patrick's Armour*, Dublin 1880.

Sarah Davies, *Wanderers Brought Home*, Dublin 1871.

Sarah Davies, *A Helping Hand*, Dublin 1881.

Rev Alexander Dallas, *The Story of the Irish Church Missions*, London 1867.

Rev A. Dallas, *A Mission Tour Book in Ireland*, London 1860.

Rev A Dallas, *The Point of Hope in Ireland's Present Crisis*, Hants 1849.

Mrs Dallas, *Incidents in the Life and Ministry of Rev. A. Dallas*, Nesbit 1871.

Caroline Cornwallis, *The Philosophy of Ragged Schools*, London 1851.

Thomas Guthrie, *Out of Harness*, Strahan 1867.

Irish Church Missions Annual Reports, London 1853-1878.

Irish Church Missions Year Book 1931, London 1931.

A. E. Hughes, *Lift Up a Standard,* London 1948.

Fitzpatrick, Hayman, Murray, *What Ireland needs,* 2nd edition, London 1880.

Kathleen Villiers-Tuthill, *A History of Clifden,* 1810-1860, Galway 1981.

Dublin Historical Sketch, London 1852.

G. Drought, *Coombe Boys' Home,* 1875.

Jane E. Whately, *Life and Correspondence of Richard Whately,* London 1886.

Rev Dr Cahill, *Sacriligious Conduct of the Coombe Soupers.*

Letter from Rev. E. McCabe, Dublin 1857.

Rev Dr Cahill, *Sacriligious Conduct of the Coombe Soupers; Letter from Rev. E McCabe,* Dublin 1857.

Rev Dr Cullen, *Pastoral Letter,* (n.d.).

'A Catholic Clergyman', *Cardinal McCabe,* 2nd edition. Dublin 1885.

Desmond Bowen, *Souperism-Myth or Reality,* Cork 1970.

T. P. O'Neill, *Sidelights on Souperism,* Dublin 1948.

Peadar Mac Suibhne, *Cardinal Paul Cullen,* Vol. III, Naas 1965.

Margaret Gibbons, *A Prisoner for the Poor,* Dublin 1967.

Attic Press presents

PERSONALLY SPEAKING: Women's Thoughts on Women's Issues, Liz Steiner-Scott (ed)
£5.95 (pb)   £12.95 (hb)

"**Personally Speaking** is a time bomb, and it is the only kind of bomb I can imagine ever having a creative and positive outcome ... It has already become my handbook and whether I open it in the garden, in the bath or on top of the bus, I feel I am in the company of women who understand and with whom I emphathise."

June Levine, *Southside*

"To be honest I thought it was just another woman's book until I burned the midnight oil reading many of the contributions ... However, this is different — 22 different women writers, of all ages, background and opinions have been skilfully gathered together between the covers of this new book and it is at once provocative, interesting, annoying and gives a marvellous picture of how Irish women feel about a variety of topics."

Maureen Fox, *Cork Examiner*

"At last we have the beginnings of a native feminist anthology."

In Dublin

IRISH WOMEN'S GUIDEBOOK & DIARY 1986
£2.95 (pb)

The **Irish Women's Guide Book and Diary** is here again and with it plenty of information, facts and fun. The 1986 Guide Book documents some of the support available to women interested in setting up their own business; participating in government or semi-state schemes; training or retraining. It highlights the eligibility criteria and points to those areas which discriminate against women because they are women. If you want to know what is available for women in Ireland then the **Irish Women's Guide Book and Diary 1986** is your starting point.

There are almost 150 new entries in the directory section, providing the most comprehensive and up-to-date list of contacts for women in Ireland — a perfect resource for anyone involved or interested in information about women's; community or related groups and organisations.

Your annual quota of cartoons, books, photos, unusual and amusing quotations, menstrual chart, important dates and much more are also here.

For 1986 catalogue send SAE to Attic Press

Back Titles

SMASHING TIMES: A History of the Irish Women's Suffrage Movement
Rosemary Cullen Owens £4.95 (pb) £10.00 (hb)

"This is a book which urgently needs to be read by anyone interested in the foundation of modern Irish Society."
> Lucille Redmond, *Sunday Press*

"A most enjoyable and worthwhile book both for the historian and general interested reader."
> Mary Leyden, *Roscommon Champion*

Smashing Times brings to life the women of the nineteen hundreds who were active and militant suffragettes. It is a remarkable and rewarding account of the Irish Women's Franchise League who fought for women's right to vote.

*DID YOUR GRANNY HAVE A HAMMER???
Rosemary Cullen Owens (ed) £3.95 (pack)

"A cheeky challenging title of a history of the Irish Suffrage Movement from 1876-1922. It is not a book like any other to me that seeks to write women back into history. It is meant to whet your appetite and encourage you to ask about your granny, and wake you up with a wink, a laugh and a nudge to the fact that women were up and about and doing, way back then."
> Nell McCafferty, *In Dublin*

This wide ranging and informative pack consists of 26 items, entertainingly presented and fully illustrated. An unusual feature of this pack is a facsimile of the *Irish Citizen* — an eight page special edition which includes leading articles taken throughout the paper's existence from 1912 to 1920.

*MISSING PIECES: Vol. 1 £2.00 (pb)

"One of a promising series, *Missing Piecess* covers the period from the famine of the 1840s. It has a wide spectrum and covers women from the arts, politics and sports." *Irish News*

*MORE MISSING PIECES:
Her Story of Irish Women £2.95 (pb)

". . . resurrects more forgotten Irish women like the sorceress who indicted a bishop for defamation of character; the medical student threatened with excommunication should she continue her studies; the Cork woman who was a pirate; and the hang-woman of the Assizes, among others."
> Nell McCafferty, *In Dublin*

More Missing Pieces is a colourful patchwork of over sixty Irish women's lives, adventures and exploits. It is a book with a difference.

Back Titles

RAPUNZEL'S REVENGE
Fairy Tales for Feminists

. . . . and they all lived happily after.' Or did they? It's a bit different down in the woods today, with Goldilocks squatting in the Three Bears' house, the Plastic Princess joining a commune and all the princesses and heroines deciding to re-write their own fairytales.

Rapunzel's Revenge is a book which questions some of the assumptions underlying traditional fairy tales. If you've ever cringed at the gullibility of Red Riding Hood or doubted the innocence of Snow White, then this is the book for you.

ISBN 0 946211 18 3 £3.50pb

THE BEST OF NELL
A Selection of Writings over 14 Years.
Introduced by Eavan Boland.
Nell McCafferty

In this book, Nell McCafferty, well known in Ireland as a journalist and television personality, gives her own unique perspective on Irish Society. Divided into six sections which span fourteen years of her writing, Nell opens the book by recalling her early childhood experiences in Derry; draws us into the world which allowed the death of Ann Lovett to occur; deals sensitively with the long drawn out tragedy of the north of Ireland as well as outraging us with her bawdy satire.

At times outrageously funny, often angry, sometimes satirical, *The Best of Nell* is always entertaining.

> *The claim made by this title is justified. Gulped at one sitting these pieces are not only passionately partisan, but also eloquent with the pure fire of a radical anger . . . . She belongs to a minority; the most exclusive one; people who can write.*
>
> Elgy Gillespie

ISBN 0 946211 05 1 £9.50 hb   ISBN 0 946211 10 8 £3.95 pb   *Irish Times* 24 November 1984.

Back Titles

Singled Out:
Single Mothers in Ireland

Singled Out is a book written by women in Cherish, (an association of single parents), presenting realistic and practical information about single mothers in Ireland.

It provides food for thought on many issues including social attitudes past and present, employment and retraining, social welfare, housing and day care.

It is an essential source book for students, teachers, parents and social policy makers.

pb £1.95 ISBN 0946211 03 5
0950888 30 3

WHO OWNS IRELAND; WHO OWNS YOU?

Who Owns Ireland; Who Owns You is the first book of its kind to be published in Ireland. It is a unique presentation of facts and figures on living in Ireland in the 1980s. Information relevant to you is catalogued throughout in an easy accessible form, using cartoons, photographs and graphs, along with an easy to read text which both poses and answers questions you've often asked.

Who Owns Ireland; Who Owns You is not just a reference book, but will provide you with information, previously only available in highly technical or expensive format. Facts, often only fleetingly grasped through newspapers or television are now available to be drawn on and retained for use as a back-up to any argument or point you may wish to make.

Make up your own mind about *Who Owns Ireland; Who Owns You.*

Did you know:-
A child of a professional person has a 450 times better chance of a 3rd level education than the child of an unskilled labourer. – Garret Fitzgerald to UCD student, I. Times October '84.

The government only gives £5,000 to Simon Community for care of homeless and yet gives £89,000 to provide shelter for dogs.

47% of Irish manufacturing industry is foreign-owned. – Aspect Magazine. Dec/Jan '84/'85.

There are 75,000 people mainly women in Ireland using tranquillizers. Over 50 million pills are consumed annually at a cost of £12m.

Ireland has 1 policeman for every 309 people – only n. Ireland has a higher ratio within Europe.

ISBN 0 946211 19 1 £3.95pb

Attic Press
Announces
An exciting new title

A WOMAN TO BLAME
The Kerry Babies Case
Nell McCafferty

*The book that goes right to the heart
of the Kerry Babies Case.*
Irish Press

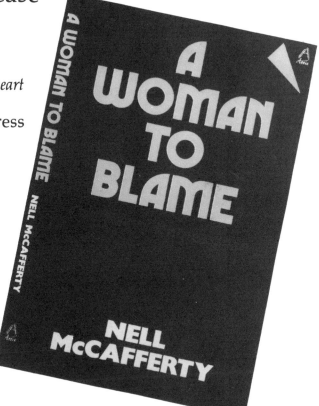

£3.95pb/ 30 b/w illustrations.

FAMILY TREE

Why not use this space to draw your own family tree.